The Accidental Producer

T0274940

The Accidental Producer

*How Anyone Can Get
Their Show on Stage*

Tim Johanson

methuen | drama
LONDON • NEW YORK • OXFORD • NEW DELHI • SYDNEY

METHUEN DRAMA
Bloomsbury Publishing Plc
50 Bedford Square, London, WC1B 3DP, UK
1385 Broadway, New York, NY 10018, USA
29 Earlsfort Terrace, Dublin 2, Ireland

BLOOMSBURY, METHUEN DRAMA and the Methuen Drama logo are trademarks of
Bloomsbury Publishing Plc

First published in Great Britain 2023

Cover design: Ben Anslow
Cover images: Black arrows icons in hand drawn style
(© MicroOne / AdobeStock); Set of hand drawn x marks (© Milano M / Shutterstock);
Highlighting Circle (© jayk7 / Getty Images); Circle Markers Animated stock video
(© Ugur Karamuk / iStock); Black paint vector circle (© Miloje / Shutterstock)

A catalogue record for this book is available from the British Library.

ISBN: HB: 978-1-3503-3833-3
PB: 978-1-3503-3832-6
ePDF: 978-1-3503-3835-7
eBook: 978-1-3503-3834-0

Typeset by Deanta Global Publishing Services, Chennai, India
Printed and bound in Great Britain

To find out more about our authors and books visit www.bloomsbury.com and
sign up for our newsletters.

For Otto

CONTENTS

ACKNOWLEDGEMENTS

This has been a labour of love and I owe a lot of thanks.

In particular to my contributors, Rachel, Jez, Paula, Justin, Alex, Heather, Chloe, Steve, Marc, Francesca and Kevin, I am hugely grateful for your time and wisdom.

To Vicky, Celia and Adam for your expertise, counsel and encouragement.

To Anna and all at Bloomsbury for your care, support and for letting me do this.

And to Charlotte, without whom I'd neither be a producer nor would have started to write this. And who I adore.

Introduction

As I pass a decade of making theatre professionally, one conclusion is inescapable. I've made a lot of mistakes.

A lot.

Some of them were dreadful. Some of them, not so bad. But boy, have I made mistakes.

Mistakes are part of learning, and when you're doing something as wide ranging as putting on a show, they're inevitable. These days I try to make sure they're always *new* mistakes. I give myself a free pass on new mistakes, they happen. When I repeat mistakes, then I give myself a hard time. But here's the thing – most of the mistakes I've made have been avoidable. Or, at least, predictable by someone who's been there before.

I spend a lot of time meeting with artists and helping them work out how to get their show on. Writers, directors, actors have a show they want to put on, and decide that they need a producer. They write to me and no doubt others.

But there aren't many producers. Not really. There are even fewer producers starting out their career, because most producers start as something else: an actor, a director, stage manager or perhaps a writer. So, given it's almost certainly not the right project for me (simply by weight of probability), I offer advice on how to do it themselves.

Nine months later I hear that the show's happened. Which is great. And then I hear about the mistakes they've made. And I think, I could've helped with that, it just didn't come up in the hour we spent chatting.

So I started writing this, detailing my advice, and informed by my mistakes. Because, the secret is:

Producing isn't that complicated.

Anyone can do it. You need good organization, to be a salesperson, and have a burning desire to get your show on. Then you just start. And hopefully people like me can help to guide you away from the mistakes we made, in the hope that you can make only new mistakes.

How I started

I began my career general-managing a show at the Finborough Theatre in London. I had done a bit of 'producing' at university, but this was my first professional production. I. Did. Not. Have. A. Clue.

A friend of mine had raised the money, and wanted me to make it happen. I ran about like a headless chicken, but my instincts, plus an experienced and patient director got me through.

I moved on to solo produce my first show at the Southwark Playhouse nine months later. A director I knew managed to secure a slot to do a revival of a well-known playwright's work (Conor McPherson's *Port Authority*). We agreed to make it happen together. I'd raise the money and he'd find the team. We were twenty-four, completely naïve and then, incredibly lucky. We persuaded actor and comedian Ardal O'Hanlon to be in it, and suddenly the industry was interested. Our careers began.

I went on to work across the small venue landscape across the UK, and once, in New York. I grafted at the small scale, and used the knowledge and relationships established at the coal face to move into a position where six-figure budgets are the norm, and the hoped-for lifetime of a show is ten to fifteen years. Who knows if I can continue to pull it off, but the mistakes made at the smaller scale will be integral to any future success I may have.

At least I feel I could now produce at that small scale and make relatively few mistakes. Or at least only new ones.

Who's this for?

If you can persuade a top producing house to put on your show, then *please* go and do that. Equally, if you have the financial resources to hire a West End theatre, general manager and team, then this isn't aimed at you. Go have fun in the West End. And maybe let me know if you'd be interested in investing. . .

This is aimed at everyone else. Those of you who are passionate but hitting a brick wall with the established venues and producers. Emerging producers and directors who want to make a name in their own right or actors who want to do something bold and different to get themselves noticed. Because anyone can produce. Sonia Friedman and Cameron Mackintosh were stage managers. Nica Burns was an actor and then a director. They all started somewhere else.

Producing only becomes complex without time or money. If you can manage both of those, you'll be fine.

What am I going to have to do?

Broadway producer Amy Danis once wrote that a producer was a banker, a cheerleader and a firefighter. Which is true. But Amy clearly wasn't talking about producing at this scale.

At small scale, a producer is a banker, a cheerleader, a firefighter, an administrator, a casting director, a press rep, a marketing agency, a launderette, assistant scenic artist, programme seller, bookkeeper, emergency stage manager, emergency lead actor, emergency director, emergency. . .

You're going to be in charge. You're going to have to raise the money. You're going to negotiate the rights and venue contracts. You're going to be responsible when it goes wrong. You'll get negligible credit when it goes right because people don't understand what you do. You'll manage brilliant talent, and the egos that come with that. You'll listen to people cry about their insecurities while you're shouting about how brilliant they are. And you'll love it.

You will have a show. Your show. You'll welcome audiences and watch as they come to love your show as well. You'll realize that there is no thrill like an audience laughing. You'll watch them stop moving at intense moments and learn the different types of quiet. You'll feel the complete joy of an ecstatic curtain call on press night. And you'll check your sales report at 6 am every morning to see if you've got a hit. And you'll work hard. So hard. And come out of the other side of it, and wonder where it's gone. And then you'll do it again. Because producing is wonderful.

But, *actually*. What am I going to do?

Once you get to the end of this, we will have covered:

Part I – Producing
This is the key section. This is what being a producer actually means.

- What are you going to put on?
- Where will you put it on?
- How will you pay for it?

We'll talk about producing as a juggling act, how to budget, how to negotiate agreements for the rights and the venue, and options for raising money.

Part II – Making it happen
Once you've decided what you're going to put on, you need to do it! This is the general management of the show (more on what that means to come).

- Appointing the right team members

- Managing casting
- Organizing and supporting the rehearsal process
- Supporting the design process

By the end of Part II, your show will be cast, rehearsed, and it'll have a set, costumes, lights and sound. The programme will be ready. There's only one thing missing . . . you need an audience.

Part III – Selling your show
There's no point making theatre if there's no one to watch it. 'Build it and they will come', is *not* a thing. We're going to look at:

- Achieving press coverage for your show
- Prioritizing your marketing budget
- Building a sales strategy

Together, these three strands make up your tool kit for selling tickets.

Part IV – Edinburgh Fringe and how to maximise the impact of a hit
Edinburgh Fringe – so many careers begin in Edinburgh. And it is its own specific, expensive, ecosystem.
And your career. The reason you're here is to progress your career. So, we're going to look at how you can optimize this process with that in mind.

To add some other perspectives, I have interviewed industry members to represent some of the interactions you will have on your journey. Sometimes they agree with me, sometimes they present an alternative view. Producing would be too easy if everyone just agreed with you.
I'm hugely grateful for all the contributors for taking the time to talk to me, I learnt loads from them, so hopefully you will, too.

Your technique

Stephen Sondheim said in one of his final interviews, 'Any art is a matter of a hundred thousand little decisions you make. And that's called technique: the principles behind the decisions.'[1]
He was talking about writing, but the same applies to producing. I cannot know the circumstances of every reader, so I can't offer tailored guidance for each of you. What I can do is illustrate the principles behind decisions

---

[1]https://www.newyorker.com/culture/the-new-yorker-interview/stephen-sondheim-final-interviews

you'll have to make, so you can take those principles and apply them to your situation. You can then build your producing technique.

A note on geography

I live in London and have formed much of my career here. As such most of my mistakes were made in London.

The principles apply in Birmingham, Manchester, Edinburgh, New York, Berlin, Istanbul or Timbuktu. The details may differ, but the principles remain the same. You need something to put on, you need somewhere to put it on, you need to pay for it and you need an audience to watch it.

Ready? Let's begin.

PART I

1

Who are you? And what are you doing here?!

You're here. You want to put on a show. Congratulations. It's going to be fun.

It doesn't matter whether you're an actor who wants to get seen, a writer who needs to get their first play on, a director with a great idea, a designer who's raised some money for a showcase or you actually want to be a producer and need to make a start. This book is for you. Because whatever the inspiration, you're after the same goal.

You want to start, or progress a career in the arts.

Putting on a show is a fantastic way to achieve this. There are other more traditional ways, but if you're here you've probably tried them. And by doing it yourself, you are in control. It's a great place to be.

In order to progress your career by putting on a show, you're going to need four things.

- To improve your craft. Particularly at the start of our careers we must all be focused on getting better at what we do.
- An audience. Audiences are the most important people in theatre. Without an audience you'll have nothing. Try to remember that throughout the producing process.
- Critics. Critical response gives you justification for your efforts. You can use the quotes to help generate an audience, to bring in the industry and as a legacy for the rest of your career.
- The industry. Critics and audience members don't control the rest of your career. The industry does. Be it venues, producers, casting directors, agents, directors or anyone else, these are the people who will allow you to progress.

To do it, you're going to be a producer. Yes, you. You, the director, actor, writer, student, lawyer, carpenter, mechanic or whoever you are, *you* are going to be a producer. It's exciting.

What is a producer anyway? Is that the same thing as the director? (Questions you'll get used to answering at family occasions . . .)

'Producer' is used across industries to mean a whole range of things. It means different things in theatre, television, music and film. Even within theatre it's used for a range of jobs. There are similarities between them, but for the remainder of this book I will be working to the following definition.

The producer is the person who has raised the money and is the driving force on the project. They are ultimately responsible for all aspects of the project, in particular, everything financial.

This is distinct from the general manager, who is often mistaken for the producer. A general manager does all of the administration, but is not actually in charge.

This is the commercial theatre definition of the two roles and is key to understand, even though when starting out, they're often done by the same person. In the not-for-profit sector some producers are general managers, some work in development, some might be producers by my definition. But it varies!

Why is this important?

If you have a second role within the show (you're the director, say), then you may look elsewhere for a producer to come and help you. But whoever they are, it's not going to be their show. It's yours. You came up with it and you're calling the shots. So, *you* are the producer. They are the general manager.

Give people whatever title you like, but unless they are taking responsibility for raising the money, they are not the producer. You are! And if they *are* taking responsibility for the money, then *they* call the shots.

Early in my career I was delighted to be asked to produce someone else's show. A group of actors or a director had a script they wanted to do, and needed someone to make it happen. I was flattered, accepted their offer and did my best. But when push came to shove, they had their agenda, and it didn't fit mine. I ended up 'producing' shows that I didn't believe in. We never found an audience, and the critics and industry didn't come. Disaster.

For those of you reading this who are planning on having a second role on the show, most of the work of the producer (by my definition) is done in advance of rehearsals, and after the bulk of the writing is done. So, it's possible to do both. What is difficult (basically impossible) to combine, is rehearsals and general management. By distinguishing between the two, we can employ someone to look after the administration without confusing who is ultimately responsible.

Another way I think about producing is this:

The producer should be the most passionate person on the project.

When I started out, I was in awe of the passion of writers and directors. Now, if I am not the most passionate person about a project then it's the wrong project. The producer is there at the beginning, and long after the show is closed. Creatives, actors and the production team come and go. But the producer is there for the long haul, so you'd better believe in the show.

How do we start?

You need to put three things in place, so you can 'green light' the show. You need to know what you're doing, where you're doing it, and how you're going to pay for it. It is the same thing the world over, on every scale. You might also need the director or the cast. But the core? Script. Venue. Money. (I know some shows don't have a script; the same principle applies.)

So which of them first? First script, then venue, then money. Well, sort of. You definitely can't get the venue or money without the script, that's clear enough. But how do you pay for the rights or the venue deposit without the money? And you can't get the money without the venue or the script because how can you draw up a budget without knowing the number of actors and the rent?!

Producing is a constant juggling act, but most of the time you start with what you want to put on, so we'll start there. After that, the venue and then the money. It will all require juggling, but with clear communication, trust and potentially a few white lies you'll be fine.

2

Choosing what to produce – 'The play's the thing'

A clever producer said to me at the start of my career, 'Bad scripts always result in bad shows. Always. You can also turn a good script into a bad show, but you can only produce a good show from a good script.' Or as Shakespeare put it – 'The play's the thing'.

Probably the worst moment you can have as a producer is realizing that the core material isn't good enough once it's too late. There's nothing you can do about it. It's why I'm so scared of devised work! Early in my career I produced a show for which I didn't think the script was ready, but I bought into the director's excitement. I decided that if he liked it that much, then it must be good enough. It wasn't, and it resulted in a painful run, to tiny audiences.

Your project is likely to come within these four categories:

- Established work. Revivals, classics and foreign work. These are established scripts that have been put on before. The writer is unlikely to be present.

  A benefit of producing an existing script is that you are likely to have some hook on which to sell the show – namely the writer, and the work's history. As a result, the rights will cost you more and may be harder to acquire.

- Script-based new work. Work that hasn't been seen before. The writer(s) are likely to be present.

  New work is exciting. It's the lifeblood of theatre, and producing it is great fun. However, with new work it is harder to answer the question 'Is the script good?' because you don't have any response from previous productions. You have your instincts, and hopefully some other trusted opinions, but you need to get objective feedback through the development process.

- New work where a script does not exist. Work where there will not be a script until the end of the rehearsal process, if at all. If the work has been done before and you have documentation of it, you can treat this as 'script'-based new work – you'll be able to show people what you're talking about.

  I have produced work that began as devised, but never devised in the rehearsal room in the weeks directly before presenting for an audience. I consider the risk of not knowing whether it's any good to be too big. People do it though. You are going to be raising money purely on the back of your reputation, and are likely to be restricted to raising from subsidized sources. But it is possible.

- Transfers. A production has already happened, and you move it to a different venue. You might be involved in a hit show that doesn't seem to have a future, or you might be an outsider who has seen it and wants to be involved. Some of my most successful shows have been transfers; I wish I'd realized their potential earlier in my career.

Where do you find ideas?

All my work has come from one of four sources:

- Collaborators I know
- Reading scripts
- Commissioning an idea
- Seeing a show I loved

Collaborators

You don't have to come up with every idea yourself. The number one way I've come across projects has been through collaborators. For me that's been writers or directors bringing me scripts, or seeing their work at a showcase.

If someone you think is talented and that you trust approaches you about a project and you like the script – ideal. If you're chatting to someone you want to work with and you go find the project together – lovely. If that person has more contacts and credits than you, so much the better!

Reading scripts

If you're working in a script-based form, you have the advantage of being able to read many scripts, relatively quickly, and get a feel for what you want to do.

Where do you find a script? Anywhere. Buy books of scripts and read. Go to a library and spend a day discovering new writers. Write to emerging writers you like and see if they've got any unproduced scripts. Ring literary agents and see if they'll send you some scripts. Ring venues and see if they have any new scripts. Read, read, read.

Commissioning work

A common way work is created is by commissioning work. It is less common on the smaller scale due to the amounts of money required. That said, it does happen. I've commissioned a number of pieces of work over the years.

A commission is when you pay an artist to create a piece that you will own the rights to for a period of time once they're finished. It will cost you more than optioning an existing script, but you'll have a greater financial stake in the rights and own them for longer.

The idea for the piece could be yours, or you could find a writer with an idea that you love and you want to support them writing it. If it's your idea, bear in mind that you need the writer to become as passionate about it as you are, or else they're unlikely to do a good job. I've found that commissioning other people's ideas works better.

Existing shows

Transferring work from a smaller venue to a larger one is common for producers. They will have already seen the show in front of an audience and know that people like it. If you're not a producer but are involved in a show that you think is great, but is only going to have a limited run, why shouldn't you approach whoever made it about taking it on?

I saw a show called *The Wasp* at Hampstead Downstairs in London and thought it could transfer to a small venue in the West End. At the time Hampstead Downstairs didn't allow critics to review. The show was fantastic and I thought it would be great to have an established show to remount and invite critics. Having Hampstead's brand attached gave the production a credibility boost I couldn't have provided. For them, their show got a further life; it was good for the reputation of their studio, future funding applications and their artists. Everyone won.

How can you tell if it's good enough?

When you're looking for a project the most important question you need to answer is 'is it good enough?' There's no faster way to kill the potential of a project than by starting out with a bad one. It can be hard to trust your instincts early in your career. But that's exactly what you must learn to do.

The job of theatre is to entertain first, everything else second. If you don't make something entertaining, the audience won't come. They don't pay money to spend their evening being lectured.

However, the great thing about entertainment is, once people are entertained, they'll take on any message you want to give them. Some of the best theatre has something important to say, a new perspective on the world or an unseen exposé. But it does that while understanding that first it must entertain. Boring is the death of theatre. Don't be boring!

What does this mean practically?

- Is it surprising?

   Surprise is at the heart of entertainment. You don't laugh at something you know is coming. It's not dramatic if you know what's happening next. Good horror is quite literally surprising.

- Is the storytelling clear?

   If you're confused at any point – the audience will be, too. Clarity of storytelling is vital.

- If it's a script, is it un-put-down-able?

   Chances are that if a script has you gripped from start to finish, you stand a chance of making an entertaining show. It is not enough for it to have just a good beginning or end, or a good premise. If it's not gripping as a read, it won't be engaging on stage. (If you don't believe me, go and read some classics – *The Crucible*, *The Importance of Being Earnest*, *The Glass Menagerie* – they're great reads.)

Remember clearly how you feel the first time you experience a story, as you'll never be able to repeat it. That first sensation of not knowing what happens and being taken in by the story is the closest you will get to what an audience will feel. As soon as you know what happens, it will never have the same impact again. So if the first time it made you laugh, then it *is* funny, even if subsequently you can't remember why!

I've produced a number of shows where I had specific doubts about a script beforehand. Every time I thought they'd be ironed out. Every time they weren't. If something in your gut says, 'I don't think this is very funny', or 'the third act is too long', then that *will* be the case on stage. For established scripts that you can't change, find a different one. For new work, you can work with the writer to improve it. More on development shortly.

If you don't have a script, then you need to find a way to experience what you're making. A workshop, or short engagement somewhere. Your instincts will be just as important here. If you can raise the money to simply trust your collaborators to make something brilliant, then that works, too. Just make sure you *really* trust them.

Other tips for script-based work

If you're looking at an existing script, research how well previous productions went. If it's had great productions in the past, you've got a good one: the script has already been proven. If it didn't have a good reception, that doesn't mean it's not a good show (remember, good scripts can result in bad shows), it just means you're going to have to have particular courage in your convictions that the script is brilliant.

A neat way of reducing the risk of the script being poor and yet it still being exciting and new to your audience is to look abroad. Are there plays that are established in their home country but not yet premiered in yours? You can trust that the script is good (if the reception was good originally), but know that it will be new to everyone seeing it where you are.

Other considerations

Finally when you're considering what to produce,

- Think from the beginning about how you are going to work with a diverse group of people across the project. Some scripts, particularly older ones, make this harder than others. It's an essential part of making work – so start thinking about it early.
- If you're choosing between a couple of ideas as an artist, please, *please,* choose the one that's going to be a great show, not just a great showcase. It will always work out better to have a less showy role in a successful piece. If the show's a dud, that's what people remember, and it's so much harder to get others to come and watch.

Developing the project

From the moment you decide on a project you will need to be developing it. Refining the piece until it's the best it can be. If you have a script you can alter, then that will be the major focus. If you don't, because it's devised, or it's a revival where you can't change the script, then this is about building the team, and the story surrounding the project, to be the most attractive to a venue.

The specifics of development, particularly of new work, could fill another 300 pages. Working with creatives to take an idea to an end product is super-exciting. It's also time-consuming and inefficient. Not all ideas make good shows, so if you're going to start based on just an idea, be prepared, you've a risky road ahead. If you spend a year developing a single idea and it's not good enough at the end of it, you're a year down the road and will have to start again.

Having said all that, I *love* development. It's so satisfying working on something brand new.

Readings and workshops

The majority of development centres on exposing the work in a controlled environment to small audiences through workshops or readings. These range from the writer and director sitting in a room reading through a script, to a musical company of thirty getting together for three weeks in a rehearsal room.

The phrases *workshop* and *reading* are often used interchangeably, but they are different. The key is to know exactly what output you're looking for. I define readings and workshops as follows:

- A reading is an event where the piece is read/performed in full. The main goal is to hear or see the show from start to finish.
- A workshop is a period of time, probably in a rehearsal room, where the creatives can experiment with the piece. There may be some sort of presentation of the results at the end, but that is not the priority. It is crucial that the creatives can pull the piece apart and make changes, safe in the knowledge they don't have to put it back together completely within the set time.

They provide a good deadline for creatives to work to, and a good opportunity to test out potential collaborators, be that the cast or other creatives (musical director/choreographer etc.). There are further pros and cons to them both.

Workshop

Pros

- Creatives love them, particularly for complex work.
- They are essential for developing devised or other non-script-based work, where the creative process is based around people being in a room together.

Cons

- They (usually) require more time and people than readings. Consequently, they can be expensive.
- Without an audience at the end, you don't get the opportunity to have venues or funders to see the piece.

Readings differ slightly depending on whether you're inviting an audience or not.

Readings without an audience

Pros

- Cheap. You might not even need actors.
- You can get loads from just hearing a script aloud.
- You can hold them anywhere – around a kitchen table, over a video call or in a rehearsal room.
- It still provides a deadline for everyone to hit.

Cons

- There are no new eyes and ears on a project. You don't have the reaction of an audience. If you've been working on it for a while, it can be helpful to get new perspectives.

Readings with an audience

Pros

- They provide an opportunity to invite key people who might help you move the project forward. In particular, funding and venues.
- If it's a play, it can be cheap: you can get actors just for one day. Musicals are much more expensive if you need the actors to learn the music. Consider having actors read and a writer sing. Or using pre-recorded tracks. Though nothing beats having actors perform.
- They provide an opportunity to get external creative feedback on the piece.

Cons

- It's pressurizing to have the industry come. People will engage in a project only once, so if it's not ready when they first experience it, that's your shot gone. I'd be more comfortable exposing something to an audience of family and friends than the industry. Just watch their reactions *as they're experiencing it,* not what they say to you once it's done. Do they all laugh at the same time? Are they fidgeting, or looking at their phone/watch? Or are they totally engrossed waiting to see what comes next?
- Industry audiences (broadly) don't laugh. They're difficult, hostile environments. I highly recommend environments where the industry are a minority, particularly if your show hopes to make people laugh.

Securing the rights

Once you've found the perfect project, it's a great feeling.

Then you need to make sure it's you who gets to produce it. You need the rights. For existing scripts, this is pretty clear cut, the rights are owned by the writer. For non-scripted work it's murkier.

If a writer is alive, or died within the past seventy years, their work is covered by laws of copyright, and you need the right to perform their play. In return for this right, you will pay the writer a percentage of box office, known as a royalty.

Once something is out of copyright (Shakespeare, Ibsen, Oscar Wilde etc.) you can skip this!

Established script rights

Rights are distributed either by the writer's agent or by a publishing company (e.g. Samuel French), depending on the scale of the production and where you want to perform it. Contact whoever you can track down, and they'll tell you who you should be speaking to.

If the rights are available, whoever you'll be talking to will want to know:

- The theatre
- The director
- The dates

If you know this information, and the rights are available, you can ask for a simple license to produce the show. This is a relatively straightforward conversation as there are no unknowns. More likely is that you don't have a venue and dates yet, and are looking for an *option* to produce the play in your location.

Obtaining the option gives you the exclusive right to produce the play within certain parameters. For example, you might want a year's option to produce the play in your city. Nobody else will be able to produce the show in that area apart from you, during that time. You will have to pay a fee to obtain the option.

Some agents are reluctant to give options, and will give you a contract only once you know all of the details. This is not a disaster. Get them to agree in principle to some venue options. Then you can go and talk to those venues and display confidence that you can obtain the license once they offer you a slot. It's all part of the juggling act.

If you can get to the writer directly, this will all become much easier. The agent works for the client, not the other way around.

New work rights

For new work, rights should be fairly simple and inexpensive to obtain. Contact the writer and ask if you can produce their play. Meet them, sell yourself to them and develop a relationship. This relationship is the first building block of your show. When you're ready, you can start to negotiate a contract with the agent. This can be after you have a theatre lined up, if your relationship with the writer is strong.

Note that waiting to start that negotiation until you have the theatre is not the conventional approach. Convention dictates that you should option a script as soon as you decide you want to do it. I got a Stage One bursary early in my career (an amazing organization, more on them later), and used almost all of it buying rights for shows I didn't manage to produce. In hindsight, I should have built packages for a production (venue, director, finance) on the basis of conversations with the agent, rather than insisting on owning the rights before I started producing the show.

To be clear, you will not have the right to produce anything until you have a contract and have paid a license fee. However, most new writers don't mind you ensuring the project is viable first. There is a risk that they might take a shinier offer, but for me that's a risk worth taking.

Non-script-based rights

For non-scripted work you will know all the collaborators. You will probably have decided to do the work together, so there's no 'obtaining' of the rights to do. You still need an agreement about ownership. Who owns how much of what you produce? If it's a hit, it'll become important. How are you defining the director's input? The actors in the room? The writer who pulls it all together? Choreographer? There's no particular right answer, the only wrong answer is not to have an agreement.

Rights agreement

A rights agreement states that you are obtaining the right to produce the piece for a period of time within a particular territory. In return for that, you will give a percentage of your box office to the writer as a royalty.

You should expect the agent to draft this agreement, which saves you a job. They will draft exclusively from their client's point of view. They will use a standard template designed for big productions and will ask for all sorts of things that they don't need. Be prepared to negotiate.

Some points that should be included:

- The dates and the location, plus venue, if a license, or scope of venues to be included in an option.
- The royalty. Anything from 4 per cent to 10 per cent net box office depending on the popularity of the piece. 'Net' box office means box office after taxes and any credit card fees are removed, but before any

costs of the show are taken off. (The total money through ticket sales is *gross* box office, after credit card and taxes are removed it is *net* box office, and the remaining after the costs of the show are taken off is *profit*.)

You will have to pay an advance against royalties. An advance means that you will be able to hold onto royalties due to the writer, until you have recouped that advance. The official language for the contract is 'a fully recoupable, non-returnable advance against royalties' (the advance is fully recoupable from box office by you, but is non-returnable by them under any circumstances – even if you fail to produce the show).

- It must have a clause stating that the writer acknowledges they own the entire copyright in the piece. It's the writer's job to make sure they haven't plagiarized anything, not yours. This clause makes this clear, and is standard.

- You should try to get some form of ongoing option for the show beyond your run. If it's a new show, this shouldn't be a problem. For example:

  'If the producer presents ten performances on stage, they retain the exclusive UK rights to the piece for a twelve-month period in which to present another production, subject to a payment of £X.'

  This gives you some security that the agent can't sell the piece to a higher bidder once it's a hit. If they're reluctant to grant this, suggest a caveat with 'subject to writer/agent's approval'. This means that if they like the production they can give you the rights, but can't sell the rights elsewhere until they've come to see it. This option probably will cost you money, but you won't have to pay it until after the initial run is over.

- Approvals. The agent will want the writer to approve everything, whether or not the writer wants to. They should be able to approve the director. Beyond that, possibly the cast? But ideally not. The more approvals your writer has, the more problems you're presenting your director with. It doesn't mean that you're not going to ask their opinion; it just leaves you with the power to decide. And *never* give approvals on the publicity image. Writing is their area of expertise, marketing is yours.

- Billing size. They will want their client to have their names 50 per cent of the size of the title on the poster. Which your graphic designer will hate as it messes up the poster design. Suggest that their client will be *the most prominent creative billed*. That should be sufficient. If you get a big-name writer's work, you might want their name at that size, but it should be up to you in the design process, not the agent in the rights process.

- Don't be put off if the agent presents the contract as a done deal. It's a power ploy, you can always negotiate. I've had a contract posted to me before. I replied with my comments by email and suggested it might be more efficient if we continued electronically.

It's not uncommon to end up working with a writer who does not have an agent. In which case:

- See if you can find an agent to negotiate on their behalf, it's counter-intuitive, but it makes everything cleaner. You can see writer's agent Rachel Daniels' opinion on this at the end of the chapter.
- If that fails, the most important terms to agree on are the royalty, the advance and the length of time you as producer have the rights.

And most importantly

- Be fair. There are unscrupulous producers around. Don't be one of them.

Paying the option

So, now we have a problem. We have a script; we have a draft rights agreement. And the agent sends the invoice. But we haven't got the money.

Time for some juggling.

Three options:

- You pay for the option, and recoup the money from the budget once you've raised the money. This is what some producers do. It secures the rights, after which they can go venue-shopping. But it requires you to have spare cash.
- You find someone else to put up that initial money. You can then return their money commercially if the project is commercial, or you can return their money as a loan if it's not. We'll come to why this is good but hard in the raising money section. But it requires you to have supporters with spare cash. So best of all:
- You delay signing the deal. Once you start negotiating the deal, you should start finding the venue and money. You might even start this the moment you find out the rights are available. Or have spoken to a venue before you made a first approach for the rights. As long as you keep everyone updated as to what is going on, you'd be surprised how well this works.

The problem with this approach is that raising money for the first time is hard. In particular if you're going for grant funding, which takes months. So maybe you ask the agent if for 10 per cent of the option fee you could secure the rights for three months while you raise the money, and can then pay them the balance? They should take that deal.

Summary

This should be one of the best bits of producing. We're storytellers, and this is about finding the right story. You *cannot* read too many scripts. Like any muscle, you need to exercise it, you'll get quick at knowing which ones you like.

- A bad script can *never* make a good show. A three-star script can *at best* give you three-star show.
- If it's new, develop the script until it's ready.
- Be prepared to find a venue before you have the rights. As long as you know they're available and amenable to you producing it, it shouldn't be a problem.
- Negotiate the rights deal. Always.

This is a great moment, you have the script, you have the rights. Now, you're going to need a venue.

INTERVIEW WITH LITERARY AND CREATIVE AGENT RACHEL DANIELS (PART 1)

Rachel Daniels is a London-based agent, representing writers, directors, composers and more. She and I have done many deals together. She is one of the fairest in the business, which is why I like dealing with her so much.

Tim Johanson   How do you see smaller-scale theatre for your clients?

Rachel Daniels   It's frustrating. Less for writers than for creatives. For creatives, the budgets of those types of productions are prohibitively low, and creatives are just subsidizing them. For writers there is more potential because they are unlikely to have been commissioned for their shows. Therefore it's an opportunity and a platform to get their work seen.

TJ   What is it that you're hoping writers will get out of it specifically?

RD   Exposure, essentially. It's hard enough to get plays and musicals on full-stop. So, if a producer is willing to take the risk to do that, and it's a new piece that has been speculatively written, I would encourage a production, provided that I think the producer knows what they're doing.

TJ   How would you judge that?

RD   Instinct, and you don't always get it right. But having done the job, as long as I have, I have a good sense of whether somebody has some idea of what they're talking about.

TJ   And at this scale, what does it take to grant the rights for an established piece that you represented?

RD   That would be down to the writer, to a certain extent, making that choice in discussion with me and the producer. It's a different set of criteria that's more in the hands of the writer to make a judgement about whether they want it done in that context, and whether it might jeopardize the possibility for that piece in a more commercial context.

TJ   And if it's an established piece that has three productions a year, is it just a question of 'are the rights available?'

RD   Exactly. Then it's a more factual decision. The other factor that might come into play is if a director who wants to do the piece wants to do something a bit different with it. If it's a piece that's been around for a long time, the writer might think, 'well, this sounds exciting'. This is worth pursuing because it could make the play more relevant today or, it could be a really imaginative production.

TJ   Would you send scripts to people if they rang and asked?

RD   It depends who's asking me. And what their interest is. I do get

approached by, actors, directors, producers . . . more about musicals
than plays.

TJ   If, say, a director rang you up and said, I've read and loved three
plays from this writer. Do they have anything unproduced?

RD   Then yes. Then that would certainly be worth a conversation.

TJ   Would it make a difference in that instance between a director and
an actor approaching you?

RD   Probably. But then again, if an actor can say to me, 'I have this
great relationship with a venue or with a producer and we are all
looking for a piece for me', because this business is so tough for
everybody, I try to be as encouraging as possible. I keep an open mind
because that's the only way that any of us can make things happen.

TJ   I'm interested in how people can build up their own credibility.
What can someone do speculatively? Should they be writing a pitch
deck?

RD   Have a plan in general. So that the agent has a sense that you have
a clear direction. The venues that you're thinking of approaching.
The rough budget, ideas about directors, casting.

TJ   Do you think any production is better than no production?

RD   No.

TJ   Have you been to press night of a client's production and gone,
well, I wish we weren't doing this?

RD   Yes.

TJ   What's likely to be the reason for that?

RD   Probably the direction. Or badly cast. Or it could be a lack of
resource, not enough, or budgets spent badly, so creatively it is doing
a disservice to the piece.

TJ   If you liked the script and the production but nobody came to
watch. Is that a problem for your client? Do you think, at that point,
I wish we didn't do that?

RD   If it's a good production, and the writer was happy with the
creative relationship with the director, and you feel that the producer
has done everything they can to maximize the potential for the show,
I wouldn't allow the writer to think it had been a mistake. And I
wouldn't regard it as a mistake, because in that case, a production is
better than no production. Especially if it's a new piece.

TJ   Do clients ever push forward to the production when you don't
think the script is ready?

RD   It has happened occasionally where the writer has also been the
director, and the director bit of the writer thinks they can solve things
in rehearsal. And that isn't always the case. So they're not prepared
to put in the work whilst wearing their writing hat.

TJ   You can't fix something in a production that's broken in a script.

RD   Especially with musicals.

TJ   When you're doing a deal, what are you looking for with regards to advances and royalties? Is it a balance between the two?

RD   You have to mitigate for the possibility of success as an agent.

That is, it is dangerous to go into a negotiation thinking, 'Oh, well, this isn't going to go very far, so we don't have to worry too much about further down the line', because you just never know. You need to protect the writer's ability to benefit, should the show have a long and fruitful life.

In terms of advances or royalty – it should be a combination of the two. That doesn't necessarily mean that you're building in huge advances, because you have to see the other side's point of view. We are all in the same business of trying to make shows happen.

It's a balance of not setting oneself unfortunate precedents, because there is a whole body of custom and practice within our agency and across the industry that you have to be cognizant of. And you don't want a producer throwing back in your face later an example of something that you previously let go in a generous moment.

It's like any negotiation; you have to work out what your bottom line is and then be prepared to stand your ground. It's not an exact science.

TJ   How do you consider other people's work inputting into your writers' work? When it comes to ownership?

RD   The bottom line is, the writer is the writer. Should there be any input from other members of the creative team – the writer is going to be the person who's inputting that and making it work in the context of the play or the musical. So, it should be regarded as part of their copyright.

However, in musicals particularly, a director can be crucial to the development of a piece. And as a writer's agent in the context of musical theatre, I believe, subject to the degree to which this input has happened, there is an argument for a director to participate in the writer's royalty.

TJ   So just a financial arrangement? They wouldn't have any control over the rights in terms of deciding where and when it's performed. It's an acknowledgement of creative contributions to the fundamentals?

RD   Yes. I have dealt with directors wanting a share of a writer's royalties for a play. And I have more of a problem with that. With a play, there are no other elements that you need somebody outside of the writing team to try and pull it all together, which is what makes musical theatre complicated. It's a rocky road to allow directors to participate in a play.

TJ   How do you sort this out if you have clients who work in a devised or semi-devised setting?

RD That's a minefield and therefore it needs to be absolutely clear before that devising process starts what the terms of engagement are. Because I have had situations where the terms of engagement were not clear. It becomes a mess, and a lot of blood, sweat and tears to try and sort it.

TJ If you were advising a writer who was unrepresented, how would you advise people to come to an equitable arrangement?

RD The writer should seek advice. From The Writer's Guild, anybody else they know in the industry. And ideally an agent.

TJ Try to avoid that situation?

RD Yes. Because they're not going to know what to do, and they're vulnerable because they want their play done. The producer might say, well, this is all custom and practice and this is what everybody agrees. How is a writer to know, in isolation, whether that's true or not? So, I would say to a writer, just don't agree to anything, unless you've got some advice from somebody you trust. Not a lawyer, because well, lawyers are always adversarial. They're not pragmatic in the way that an agent would be hopefully pragmatic.

Continued on page 59.

3

Finding the perfect venue

Script, done. Next: Venue, budget, raising money.

Venue, budget and money need to be thought about at the same time, because they all interlink. Consider these next three chapters as running concurrently alongside each other.

We're going to start with finding the right venue.

No two venues are alike. They have different layouts, different capacities, different locations, different brands and, most crucially, different people running them.

Your market will dictate your options on choosing a theatre. There may be one option, there may be many. In my base in London there are over 140 theatres. Seventy to eighty of them might reasonably be available to hire. And that's just until you realize that you can make theatre in any space . . .

Types of venues

There are three types of venues. Ones that produce their own work, those that don't and hire it to external producers, and the ones that do a bit of both.

Producing houses

A producing house produces its own work. It tends to be not-for-profit, funded by government subsidies, patrons and grants. It is able to take risks with what it produces, in a way that is harder in commercial theatre. It trades off its reputation, building up trust with its audience such that people come to watch on the basis that the theatre is producing it, not necessarily what the show is.

Most producing houses do some receiving work produced by other people as well. Many touring venues fall into this hybrid category.

Getting your work into a producing house is hard, particularly at the start of a career. If you can, *that is a good thing*. If you are a performer who wants to be on stage, or a director needing an opportunity, that may be your ultimate goal.

Receiving houses

These are venues for hire. Some receiving houses are programmed in such a way that they maintain a particular type of work, or a particular quality, trying to build a reputation like a producing house. On the small scale, this is common. Other receiving houses will take whatever they think will sell the most tickets. The West End and Broadway come into this category, as do many small venues that don't have the luxury of curating what they present.

If you're touring a show, you will work with a series of receiving houses, unless you are co-producing with them (see in what follows).

You can also hire non-traditional spaces. Anything can be a theatre! If you've ever been to a fringe festival, you'll realize that even the smallest spaces can become performance spaces. The drawbacks are you have to start from square one – is there enough power for my lights, where are the toilets, how am I going to run a box office, etc. All things covered if you work in a traditional space.

Co-productions

Co-productions are, to me, the Holy Grail. You partner with a producing house, they make the show and run it at their venue, and then you transfer it to a receiving house somewhere.

All the rest of what I've said in this book applies to when the show gets to the receiving house, but as a co-production with a producing house, it will come with a reputation, a stamp of quality, possibly reviews, and it will probably cost you less overall. The producing house may need a contribution to the upfront costs, but the overall cost/benefit to you is huge. The benefit to them is you bringing them a show they want; their brand will move with the show, which is great for them to talk to their audiences and funders about. You will probably also pay them a royalty when you put on the show.

My biggest show to date was a co-production where I turned up at a regional venue without a meeting (though I'd suggested a time and heard nothing), bumped into the AD who was embarrassed, and two hours later had a meeting that led to the production. It's all a hustle.

It probably requires a prior relationship to pull off, but find somewhere that makes theatre and make a pitch. You never know. Persuade an artistic director to direct the show, and everything happens more easily. Do not expect it to happen fast: co-productions are usually organized twelve to twenty-four months in advance. Lots of time to get it right!

Approaching a venue

All venues are programmed by someone. Be that an artistic director, or an administrator responsible for programming, there is someone making a decision about whether you can put your show on in that space.

The key to getting them to say yes, is to work out:

- What do they like to programme?

    Some venues have a clear written artistic policy. Some you'll have to judge based on their programming.

- What is it about your project, therefore, that might appeal to them? And why is their venue the right one for you?

    For a high-class producing theatre this will have to be something exciting and artistic. For a non-traditional space for hire, this will be a far more financially led discussion. Look for artistic policies. If they're a new-writing theatre, don't waste your time trying to sell them a Tennessee Williams revival.

- What risks does your project have for them?

    Are you going to be able to deliver it, and generate an audience? How can you show them you've got it sorted?

- How are you going to tell them about it?

    This is a sales process, and as any salesperson in any industry will tell you, getting to the decision maker is the key element in making a sale.

    It may be an easy approach to the decision maker. Many smaller venues for hire are one person operations, and their email address or phone number is readily available. If you're looking to co-produce with a major not-for-profit theatre, it's going to be a heck of lot harder to get your project in front of the right person.

    Fringe festivals require a lot of content and can be the easiest place to get programmed. They tend to have formal submission processes, which do work. It's *still* a good idea to try to meet the decision maker to persuade them that your show requires programming in the best venue, in the best slot.

The one thing that all venues want is to sell tickets. Even the worst run venue wants a good show. So sell your show from the first phone call. They must understand why yours is the show they need to programme this season.

How you're going to find them a new audience, satisfy their old audience and what a big hit you're going to have. You need them to be excited about your show.

How do you know which venue to approach?

This varies depending on the type of venue.

If you're looking for a co-production, the determining factor is which venues' decision makers you can get to, to pitch your project. When starting out, other considerations are less of a concern, as getting any co-production is hard.

For venues for hire, it's more complicated. What are we looking for in a venue? Reputation. Location. Slot. Price. In that order.

Reputation is the most important. Audiences, critics and the industry are all more likely to come to a venue they respect. It trumps everything else. If you can get your show into a known producing house – amazing. If you can't, but you can persuade a top rental house to take it, then people will immediately take interest in your show. It's worth sacrificing other considerations like location, time of year and the price for the right place.

Reputation is still important with lesser-known venues. Beware a bad reputation. Much like a good one, a bad reputation trumps everything. There are a few seemingly perfect venues in central locations in London that don't ever have good stuff on. Why? The people running them, probably. Or maybe they're unpleasant places to watch theatre. Who knows? But beware.

So, if reputation is equal. What now? Think like an audience member: what would put you off going to see something? For me, the number one thing is location. Number two is time of year.

The right location means different things depending on your project. Who are your audience likely to be? Almost certainly a large proportion will come from your personal network. Therefore, a local venue might be the right venue. Particularly if you're looking for only a few performances. If in doubt, then prioritize somewhere central; if that's not possible, find somewhere close to transport links.

Then, there are times of year that are better for theatre than others. January, the summer and September are tricky. February to April and October to December are excellent. Why? In the summer I'm in the park or on holiday, aren't you? January, I'm inside saving money. September I'm working out what I'm doing now that the summer is over.

The bigger the show, the bigger a problem this is. If you're in 1,000-seat venues it's a big consideration. If it's 100 seats it has less of an impact as you have fewer seats to sell. I've seen a number of shows sell out in August. It's just harder than in March.

Price. This is fairly obvious. If all else above this is equal (with one caveat to follow), then go for the cheaper venue. But make sure the other bits are equal first!

The one caveat is to make sure you've been to your preferred venues and watched something. You should book a ticket online, and go to whatever is on. This gives you the true audience experience. A bad website makes people think that the show will be bad. A bad experience at the theatre means they won't tell their friends to go, however good the show.

The largest press coverage I ever received was an Off-West End play about Barack Obama in a London railway arch. We had a double-page feature in the Guardian newspaper that resulted in almost zero tickets, which I could not understand. Years later a West End press rep asked me what the website was like. He said the press almost certainly drove people to the website, but if it was terrible, they would bounce off. The website *was* awful.

What happens when a venue bites?

When a venue decides to do your show, it tends to move quickly. So be prepared.

There are a few things you need to decide on before you can confirm a venue.

- The length of run
- The production schedule – get-in, tech, dress and first performance
- The financial deal

Some smaller venues are not programmed far ahead and may offer you a slot that is sooner than you're expecting. Be careful, you need time to get your show right. If they say that the only one available is in three months, ask yourself why that might be and be prepared to walk away.

Once you are in agreement about the deal, they're going to send you an invoice for a deposit. It can come quickly, and they will not confirm the venue until you've paid. So, once you get a nibble from a venue, use the time spent negotiating the venue agreement to push ahead with fundraising.

How many performances should we do?

Once you find a venue, an important consideration is the length of the run. You probably need a three-week run, in order to persuade critics to come. But the more performances, the greater the risk. We'll cover this in budgeting in a minute.

Talk to the venue about their recommendations – ask about what the box office has been for shows in the past – they may not be willing to tell you exact figures, but even just ballpark averages are useful for budgeting. If in doubt, do *fewer* performances. Far better to sell out ten shows than have half houses for twenty. Be suspicious if they provide vague numbers. Find someone who's worked at that venue before and get their numbers. Other producers are likely to be far more honest.

Venue schedule

At this stage you're going to have to put the date for your access to the theatre, first preview and press night in the contract, so you need to draft a schedule for the opening week of technical and dress rehearsals, previews and press night.

Talk to your production manager and director about this, if you have them already. If you don't, you'll have to make a judgement.

The toss-up here is between giving your creative and production team a realistic amount of time to get the show ready, and the need to get an audience in to start generating box office income to offset the rent you're now paying (if you're renting the venue).

We're going to talk a lot more about tech and dress rehearsals later, but for now . . .

Presuming you get access on Monday morning:

- A Monday first show is acceptable for a show that's already had its tech run and has a minimal set. For a simple tour this is relatively common. Stand-up comedy, or an equivalent is fine.
- A Tuesday first show is acceptable where there's negligible get-in time and simple set, lights and sound. Tech has to begin by Monday mid-afternoon, finish at lunch Tuesday for a dress run Tuesday afternoon before first preview. This does happen, particularly for transfers, but is hard on your team. For touring, this is (pretty much) as relaxed as it gets on a weekly touring schedule.
- A Wednesday first show is more common. It's a realistic small-scale schedule. It will allow a decent get-in time, tech to start Tuesday first thing then dress Wednesday afternoon. It's tiring, but this allows for at least a day to get in, a day and a bit for tech and a dress rehearsal. If you can get in on Sunday, you can then have your first show on a Tuesday.
- A Thursday first show is the kindest option. There should be more than enough time to get the show to the creatives' vision. Inevitably, press night will have to be delayed to accommodate this.

On a short run (four weeks or fewer), it's vital to have press night in the first week in order to get the reviews out in time to help with ticket sales. This almost always means the Friday. This allows three previews if you open on the Tuesday, and two if you open on the Wednesday. If you're only doing a week or two's run, you may need to find a way to open on the Monday and have press night after only one preview or so.

As I work on larger shows with bigger budgets and greater lead times, what becomes clear to me is that the best work is done when there is time. With short runs it's so hard. You need to get to first preview, you need to get to press night, but two or three days in the theatre before your first show is so often not enough to deliver a professional production. What to do? Fight for more time in the venue. Preserve budgets for overnight lighting rigging or set building. Or simplify the show technically. There are always areas that need compromises, and this is one of them.

Venue contract

Your venue contract is the second major contract you're going to come across and is probably the most important. It's certainly going to be the most expensive! The good news is they will draft it for you.

The contract will state that your venue will provide the stage and technical infrastructure, will manage the box office and potentially provide some marketing and PR. You will provide the production and the core marketing materials.

There are a range of different financial arrangements in theatre. The type of run and location will narrow down what the options are. The central premise underlying all of them is, Who is going to take responsibility for selling the tickets? The venue, the producer or a combination of the two?

For a tour this deal is particularly crucial. You can't be expected to be an expert in each market in which you're taking the show, so you are reliant on each venue to sell tickets. The deal you do defines how much risk you are taking in each venue, and therefore how reliant you are on the venue's marketing department.

There are four basic deals. Let's say it costs you £600 to put on a performance, and the venue is trying to make £200.

1) They pay you to come. It's called a guarantee. They give you the £600 for a performance, and you deliver a show. All the risk is on them, which is dreamy. If you can find venues that will pay a guarantee (and a big enough guarantee), then this is worth doing. Even if they sell only £300 worth of tickets, you've already got your £600. Venue marketing departments are working hard to sell your show.

2) You agree to take the first 'call' on the box office. You take the first £600 per performance of ticket sales. They then take the next 'call' of a certain amount, say £200. And if there's more left after that then you split it. The risk is still on them, as they need to sell over

£600 worth of tickets to make anything, but the risk is shifted a bit to you, as if they sell only £300, that's all you get. Venue marketing departments are still working hard.

3) You split the box office. Generally, this will be in your favour, 80:20 or so. You need to sell £750 worth of tickets to get your £600. However, the venue is making money from minute one. If they only sell £300 in this scenario, you take home £240. Venue marketing departments are working, but not as hard, as they're making money from the first ticket sold. *On tour this is likely what venues will offer*. Ask yourself, 'What happens if they sell only ten tickets?'. If you can cover that eventuality, crack on. Venue splits are how the Edinburgh Fringe operates.

4) You rent the venue. For £200. So, you'll need to take £800 worth of tickets to cover the rent and break even. And the venue isn't taking any risk at all. Never ever do this on tour. Their marketing department will be on holiday.

In London, this is the deal you should expect to get. Then it's a question of how low you can get the rent.

If you're looking at booking a tour, understanding this and being crystal clear on your numbers is vital. In theory it is possible to organize a tour simply based on guarantees, with you taking no risk at all. But if your costs go up, your income is already fixed. A fully guaranteed tour is awesome, so long as you're absolutely on top of your numbers.

Other venue contract clauses to expect

Things to watch out for:

- If you're renting, how much of a deposit do the venues want? One week's rent is appropriate; they can take the remainder out of your ticket sales. Some smaller venues don't trust producers to sell enough tickets to cover the rent for the whole run, so they ask for the full amount upfront. If that's the case, they clearly don't have faith in you, your show, or their own audience base, and just see you as an opportunity to make money. Do you really want to work there?

  Paying the rent in full upfront will also mean you will have to raise more money. Bearing in mind that you are liable for the full period of rent when you sign the contract, it doesn't change the overall financial picture, but it's irritating to have to raise extra money.

- What technical kit they will provide. Make sure they provide you with a list, and that it is up to date. You can then provide your designers with an accurate picture of what's there. The contract should state that if it's broken, or not present at the get-in, the venue will fix or replace immediately. Your designers will be relying on it, and if it's not there, it should not cost you anything to replace.

Don't expect to be able to analyse this yourself, it'll seem like gibberish. If you don't have your designers yet, find someone who can translate it for you. Range of responses I look for/can understand: 'That kit can manage a basic design', 'You can do quite a bit with that', 'You won't even be able to see the stage'. What they're providing within the deal is important for your budgeting.

- When can you begin your get-in and what is your access to the venue until press night? Venues retain the right to use their stage for external hires during the day after press night. This is standard. However, you need access all day from the beginning of the get-in, until press night.

  I've been asked to pay for daytime access after first preview. You *absolutely* need access during the day as part of the contract, it's vital for your team to work on the show after each preview. Plus, it's in the venue's interests to have the best show possible. And if you don't do this, can I watch when you tell the director? (This would be a deal breaker for me in any venue, as an indicator of the venue's professionalism.)

  Also, it sounds obvious, but do you have to clear your set every night? It will make a big difference to the type of show you can do, if so.

- Marketing support. The venue will hopefully have an audience who go regularly, who should be relatively easy for you to sell to. But it's not always the case.

  It's important to be clear at the contract stage what the venues are going to do for you. They should have an email database – how often will your show be included on emails going out? How often will it be the lead show on the email? What percentage of the mailing list will it be sent to? All of these things affect how many people actually see your show and therefore how many might be likely to buy a ticket. If you're renting a venue this is *particularly* important to talk about at contract stage, as ultimately selling the tickets is your responsibility.

  Also, will the venue allow you to work with ticket agencies, and which ones? Will you have access to audience data? We're going to talk a lot more about this in Part III.

- Don't sign a personal guarantee. Personal guarantees make you personally liable for any losses to the venue. They negate your setting up a company (more on that later), and mean they can come after any asset you have personally if the show goes really badly. Venues shouldn't ask, and you shouldn't sign. I've never signed one. If they ask for it, it means they don't trust you.

Other smaller contractual bits (my opinions . . .):

- Overnight access (for speedier get-ins) should be allowed, but expect to be charged. For some venues this logistically isn't possible.

- Refunds. I could write an essay on this. In brief. The purchase of a ticket is a contract between *you* and the purchaser. Therefore, *you* should have final say on all refunds. The theatre will argue that it's their brand that's affected. I would suggest they should take risk on a project in order for that to be valid.

  Worth discussing in advance. Refunds should be avoided. It's so hard to make a sale. When did you last get a refund for a Beyoncé concert or an Arsenal match? Try moving people's tickets to other dates. In the case of major world events, such as during Covid-19, this policy obviously eases. The principle of moving to another date rather than refunding stands, however.

- Fifteen per cent is plenty of commission for a venue to take for selling programmes. Though good luck with that discussion!

Co-production deals

If you're doing a co-production, the deal looks completely different. It's also relatively simple! The reason is that you are trusting a venue to make your show for you. They are going to sell it to their audience, and then they keep all (or most) of the box office.

- What money (if any) are you providing to pay for the production?

  This should be as little as possible. None is common. Venues have budgets for each show already, and if you're bringing them the IP, that's usually enough. Some venues want money from commercial producers to help 'enhance' the production.

- What 'originating producer' royalty are you going to pay the venue once you take the production on?

  This varies. Ten per cent to twenty-five per cent of the amount of the writer's royalty is in the right ballpark.

- What control do you have over decisions made in the original production?

  You should have sign-off over the creative team and marketing image. Beyond that you need to trust them to make the show.

- What control do the originating producers have of what you do with their production?

  This depends on who has the rights. If you're taking the show to them, then you're trusting them to make your show, so they should trust you to take on their version of it. If they have the rights to begin with, then they're going to want continuous ongoing sign-offs and engagement, which is not a disaster.

Other bits

- They may want an ongoing right to invest in the production – which should be no problem for you.
- You're going to want a certain number of free tickets to bring stakeholders to the show – again they should understand this and help you out.

Summary

One of the things that becomes clear when you're looking for a venue is that some venues that struggle to fill their slots are desperate to have you, and other oversubscribed venues aren't. And you probably want to be at the ones that aren't. They're oversubscribed for a reason. You'll need to develop a relationship, make a compelling pitch and have a bit of luck. That being said, hit shows happen all over the place, so don't take a rubbish slot at an expensive venue if it isn't right.

- Reputation over everything.
- Think like an audience member – go and be an audience member!
- Be persistent with your approach, but always be polite, you need them to want to speak to you.
- If you can organize a co-production fantastic!
- Make sure you've got the deals and numbers nailed for touring.
- You *can* negotiate the venue deal. It's the most expensive part of your show, make sure it's right.

So now you have your hit show, you've got the perfect venue. And now? Money. You definitely need it. And you probably don't have it.

INTERVIEW WITH JEZ BOND, ARTISTIC DIRECTOR OF PARK THEATRE

Jez is the founder and the artistic director of Park Theatre, an Off-West End theatre in north London. Park has two spaces, a 200-seat space – Park200, and a 90-seat space, Park90.

Tim Johanson   When producers approach you, what are you looking for?

Jez Bond   The starting point is always reading the script. Following that, it's the producer. You've got a play, you've read it and you go, okay, this is an exciting play, maybe a powerful play, maybe a play that needs to be told today – is this producer someone who is going to execute that well? Are they going to realize those words on the page and bring them to life in a way that we can stand behind?

TJ   What are you looking for with a producer, when you've got a script that you like?

JB   Three things. One, is looking at their budget and seeing how they are resourcing something. Alarm bells will go if we read a script, know what it takes to put that on and they think they can do it for half of that. Because usually what happens is, either they can't do it for half of that, and then they run out of money. Or in fact, they do it for half of that, but the show suffers as a result.

One key place we always look is the marketing budget. That's an easy place for producers to pull from and go, 'Oh, I see we'll take another thousand pounds out there and put it somewhere'. But marketing spend is crucial. If you spend, you will get it back, generally. If you don't spend, you won't. The more you put into marketing, the more chances you have of selling those tickets.

The second thing is, will they listen? Is it a producer who think they know better, or is it a producer who you feel can have relationship with because they're genuinely asking how things work in your building, have questions about your audience, or your marketing strategies?

And the third thing I suppose is you learn over the years to have a bit of a bullshit detector and you can smell that when someone is talking the big game and they don't know what they're talking about.

TJ   How do you like to be approached by somebody you don't know?

JB   We have a submission process. And then we will read it, starting with a script, but then going okay it's got a diverse cast or whatever other things we might want to consider. That has tended to be the routine for Park90, simply because most of the producers over the last few years in Park200 are people who would be known to me and have some relationship with me and would just go, 'Hey Jez, have a look at the script'.

But the people who don't know me, if they can get an intro through someone that's helpful. We read everything that comes through our door, from a producer. Because we can't in-house produce a huge amount of work and don't have a literary team and reams of money, we don't accept unsolicited scripts where a writer just sends in a play. But again, sometimes there are writers I have relationships with for Park90 – so I have found things like that.

TJ That's a really honest answer. It's always been my experience that you can't just email the programming email address. You need to build relationships. How do you weigh up the importance of scripts versus stars versus directors?

JB That is the magic of programming! At the end of the day, it's a call that you make and there's a balance within a show and there's balances within a season and balances within a year.

TJ How important is the star?

JB Well, financially, hugely important. I always feel frustrated that that is the case, but that is the reality of the world we live in. People want to go and see a name that they recognize. It is by far the biggest & easiest hook to sell tickets.

TJ And how does programming vary between Park200 & Park90?

JB They're very different spaces. When we're talking to producers there is a different set of criteria that I look for in Park200 and Park90. And that is mainly going back to the point about how one resources a show.

Because in Park90, there may be shortcuts you can do financially that you can't in Park200. Now Park200, you need to see it more as a sort of commercial opportunity. It's got to be a show that on the face of it could wash its face and make a bit of money.

Whereas Park90 tends to be more about giving that show an opportunity there and then in that space, if we think there is an audience for it. It tends to be shows that aren't going to be resourced as well. It would be ludicrous to resource them as well because you can't get that much money back. And in fact, you will most likely lose money in Park90. We tend to have less experienced producers in Park90. And certainly, we would only ever have more experienced producers in Park200.

TJ How much flexibility do you have with the producer on ticket prices and lengths of run?

JB We are both a producing and receiving house. Because of that the audience perception and the critics' perception, is that any show is a Park Theatre show. They don't differentiate between Tim Johanson producing it or Park Theatre producing it. It's a show they've seen at

Park Theatre, so it's a Park Theatre show. And because of that, we try to ensure continuity across all shows.

Part of that continuity is ticket prices. Ticket prices are the same, no matter if you've got a big star in it, or you've got an unknown. We don't want to penalize people and say to our lovely audiences, 'Okay, you came to see this show. Now pay double if you want to see the next show', because we're building customer loyalty. That in turn passes back to the producer as we have a nice loyal audience for them.

And the other thing that has some sense of continuity is the length of runs. Slightly less important than the ticket price, because it isn't observed in the same way by an audience. We have a little bit of flexibility within it, and we tend to make that call on the show-by-show basis.

Sometimes you have a good show, but it takes a while to build that up. The last two weeks might be sold out. Then you think, 'Oh, if we did one more week, maybe it would have been . . . ', but you never know. We're not going to be a venue that just runs and runs because we're not that sort of place, but maybe we'll do an extra week or an extra two weeks, or maybe also we'll add a few extra shows during the run.

TJ   If you have producers where you have had problems, where do the pinch points come?

JB   It's either finance related or HR related. And it's because they haven't resourced the show properly, so suddenly people aren't getting paid, or the technical rehearsal is not going as it should because the set doesn't work properly because there've been compromises . . .

Or HR. We've had shows where the producer has got the show up and running and then just disappeared. It's very rare, but once or twice. There's one time I can think of where the producer was completely absent and there was an actor who was vile to the other members of staff, the other actors and stage managers, and you'd want to just fire them in the middle of a show. And as the artistic director of the building, I step in and have to deal with that. And that's a lack of experience that the producer just kind of let go of the reins.

TJ   How do you mitigate against those problems?

JB   Well, I mitigate against those problems by referring to the question you asked me earlier, which is working out the relationship with the producers? How do I suss the producers out? I'm trying to ensure that the people I work with aren't people who are going to neglect their duties, under resource their show, or let go of the reins.

TJ   It's all about that initial pitch stage?

JB   Yes, it is.

4

Getting the budget right

Money. Here we are. For most people, this is the place where they're most concerned. Which I understand. But trust me, it's *totally* doable. Every show that's been put on, in any venue ever, has managed it.

Ok, that's not true, some have been disasters. But *the vast majority* of shows manage it just fine!

First thing is to work out how much you need. You need a budget. Everything from running your home to running a government has a budget. Theatre is no different. You need to establish how much you need to spend to make the production happen, how much you can realistically bring in and then make money in equal (or exceed) money out.

You should start writing a budget as soon as you've chosen what you want to put on.

Three principles of budgeting before we go into more detail:

- There is not going to be enough money to satisfy everyone, and it's going to be a constant battle to make it work.

  The only show I've worked on outside of the West End that had truly enough money to satisfy everyone was paid for by a wealthy actor who wanted to use it as a showcase. The expenditure ended up four times larger than the income. The actor could afford it, and everyone's fee and budget exceeded their expectations. But that's unlikely to be you and your situation.

- Your budget should be constantly updated to reflect new knowledge. Start with something, *anything*, and continually improve with every conversation you have, until it is as accurate as possible, and you're ready to green-light the show.

- Find people that know more than you in your market to help. Ask your director for help, ask the venue you're talking to, approach other producers and ask them to look at the budget. However you can, get external feedback. It's the only way to achieve accuracy.

The process

Start by having a guess at the expenditure. Then pick a venue you're looking at, and have a guess of your potential income. Then get some information and refine your expenditure. Then start chatting to venues, and refine your income. Eventually you'll get to a point where you're confident you're in the right ballpark with both. Then you can work out whether income might equal expenditure or whether you'll need subsidy.

If you're touring, you can go through a similar process, but rather than picking a single venue, use your expenditure to work out how many dates you're going to need to do, and how much income you're going to need from each, in order to make the tour 'viable'. And then you need to work out if that's realistic (100 date tours work on paper, but are probably not realistic to organize).

Expenditure

Your expenditure is going to be split into four broad categories.

- People – the most expensive part of your budget.
- Production costs – set, costume, lighting, sound, props, video etc.
- Marketing/PR – the easiest bit to forget about, but extremely important.
- Other – administration costs, insurance etc.

Creative team

Let's begin with the creative team. These are your director, your designers, choreographer etc. The creative team is a variable section of the budget. Who knows how much people cost?

One of the complexities is that, along with the actors, they are most likely to get non-monetary value from the project through press coverage and inviting industry (compared, say, to the stage management). As such, there are ulterior motives for getting involved in smaller-scale work.

There are a few ways to approach it.

- Look at union agreements and try to get as close as possible. (I've often done this.)
- Talk to the artist or the agent as to what they think is reasonable. (I've rarely done this.)
- Start with a day rate and estimate how much time they are going to put in. (I've usually done this.) Your lowest legal day rate is

determined by minimum wage; the higher you go above that, the less of a fight you'll have, and the less guilty you'll feel.

Crucially, whatever approach you decide to take, you're going to have to justify it to the artist and agent. So better to have a logic behind it, than picking a number out of thin air.

There is a convention with creative teams that the director is paid a bit more than the set and costume designer, who in turn is paid a bit more than the lighting designer and the latter a bit more than the sound designer. Poor sound. I use this structure, but pay sound the same as lighting. I don't know where the convention comes from – maybe it's historically based on the amount of time put in? But if you're struggling with a set designer negotiation, mentioning that the director is being paid X, and you can't therefore go above Y, is quite a good way to finish the negotiation.

The director is a tricky one as they've often been in from the start. They might be part of the producing entity (see profit share section coming shortly). Even if they're not, they're going to put in a lot of work. Equally, they're going to get the most out of it in terms of reputation, every review will talk about them.

Determining their time put-in is particularly hard. As a minimum, castings, rehearsals, tech and previews. Plus, a bit for the endless meetings, site visits, other areas the director will input in.

Designers are invaluable, but they can take on more than one job at a time. Work out the time required with them and their agent. If they could make it work in only a couple of days and some prep, you'd be surprised what you can get. A regular response to a lower fee is, 'You will only have me until first preview'. Talk to your director about how disruptive that might be, and make a decision together.

Casting directors are useful. Their job involves expertise and legwork. If you do the legwork, their expertise can come at a reasonable cost. Get in touch and ask for a quote, then ask how you might reduce the quote, while still getting their help. More on working with casting directors in Part II.

You do not *have* to have all these creatives if you can't afford them. One show I worked on was just two chairs and a piano. Why? Because they couldn't afford a designer, so the director got two chairs and said, 'That'll have to be our set'. Another show I came across, the writer, produced, directed, did the set and lighting design, built the set, did the publicity image and more. He then made up a load of pseudonyms in the programme as he thought it would look like a vanity project if he took credit for everything he'd done. Very few people could do that, but as an experienced maker, he knew that he couldn't afford anyone else, and he came up with a solution.

I do not recommend you copy that approach. Better the one where you just don't have the elements you can't afford. But included to show how people make it work!

Production team

The head of the production team is the production manager. They are almost essential, and the good ones are expensive. Find out who they are (ask venues, other producers, artists) and just start asking if they'll do it. You might well find an emerging one for not too much money. This is somewhere worth spending, though. A bad production manager and you'll just see the production budget costs rise to accommodate their inadequacies. I would expect to pay the production manager similarly to the director on most shows.

If you need a physical fight, a fight director is required. Likewise if your script requires physical intimacy between performers, an intimacy coordinator will need to run a session or two. A dialect coach is a luxury, likewise an assistant director. For all of the aforementioned, ask for a quote – they tend to charge on a day-rate basis.

For a musical you have more essential appointments. A musical director (pay as actors during rehearsals and run, and further if they're working in advance), a choreographer (pay roughly the same as a designer) and an orchestrator (similar to the total musical director fee? They are pricey). You can see how musicals become expensive.

Actors, stage management and band

It's good to separate creatives from actors, stage management and band. The crucial difference is the amount of time they each have to put in and their exclusivity to your project. From a budget perspective this is pretty easy. Decide how much you're going to pay on a daily/weekly basis, pay them all the same and put it in the budget.

Paying all the same is key. Instinct suggests that lead actors should be paid more, and maybe the assistant stage manager (ASM) the least. Not until you're working at considerable scale. Even then, it's only at a West End or major touring level that they earn varying amounts. For you, they all give up the same amount of time (or at least can't take on another job for the same length of time), so they should all be paid the same.

Paying people the same is known as 'favoured nations', or 'most favoured nations'. I've no idea why, but it's baffling hearing agents mention it for the first time.

Be aware that band members have a convention of 'depping': if they can't make a certain performance, they find someone to replace them. It's standard practice, and they sort out the money themselves, you just pay the original person. It seems to work fine!

You'll quickly work out that after the venue – this is the most expensive section of any budget. Which is why the industry has spent a lot of time talking about profit share.

The big mess that is profit share

Over my career one phrase has dominated discussions around small-scale theatre: profit share. It's a complicated and divisive issue. One to tread around carefully and with your eyes wide open. What is profit share?

Well, exactly that. The idea that you share any profits from a project with the company members at the end. It's not just a theatre thing, it's something that major corporations have. UK retail giant John Lewis has a famous profit share with every member of its staff. The key difference with theatre is that all of John Lewis' staff have an acceptable base salary, and are partners in the decision-making.

There is a history, particularly in fringe theatre, of paying everyone a token amount for their expenses and then the whole company split any profit at the end. You go through the motions of making a production, actors come to audition, you find stage management who are looking for contacts and a credit, you can probably even find a production manager if you look hard enough. Everyone gets to work, everyone gets a credit on their CV, everyone builds a relationship with one another, no one was forced to do it – everyone wins, right? Because, boy, will it make your budget look more viable!

Well. Not quite. Some people (you, the director, the writer if the show's new, possibly the lead actor), benefit from the project more than others, which starts to look a bit like exploitation. Put into the mix that the people that benefit the most are also the people making the decisions, and it looks even worse. Also, if one in ten shows ended up paying out any profit I'd be amazed. So really, profit share is cover language for 'not paying people'.

This is such a big discussion that it has ended up in an employment tribunal. While the tribunal ruled that actors are self-employed contractors and therefore profit share was not illegal, it's not controversial to say that the industry disagrees.

Union agreements

There is literature dictating how much you should pay people. These are agreements between theatre members associations and the unions (Equity,

BECTU, Musician Union etc.). They have rules that members of those organizations must abide by in order to maintain their membership.

You are not obligated to use any of the agreements unless you are a member of one of those associations, or working in a theatre that requires all producers to abide by an agreement they are part of. However, they are a useful guide for industry standards.

Acceptable profit share

There is one situation where profit share is absolutely fine. If you, say, a writer, and a friend, a director, decided to produce a show. In that instance you are both the producers and neither of you needs to pay the other anything. You can agree in advance that you'll both work hard to get the show on, and at the end split whatever's left. You then pay everyone else who comes on board.

I have a group of three actor friends who produce their own work. They pay everyone else involved, but work themselves for free if the budget requires it. Then they split anything left over at the end. Absolutely fine.

If you sit down with a group of people and collectively decide to do a show together, then you are under no obligation to pay anyone within your group any more or less than you all decide. But that is the key. That you *all* decide. The power is shared equally, and you've all bought in at the same time and level.

As an independent producer, this isn't something I've ever done, but I suspect that anyone coming on board after you've signed the venue contract probably couldn't be considered to have been part of the decision-making process.

Whatever you do, consider open-book accounting. It allows anyone involved to see the budget and accounts. It allows transparency that no one is getting screwed. It also is a useful way of people understanding how hard keeping on top of costs for a show can be.

That first show I produced I paid the actors and it went on to make money. The second show I did was (regretfully) a full profit share. It lost a lot of money. I decided then that profit share wasn't the answer to a successful show! Taking the decision to not engage with profit share since has provided some limitations for shows I can produce – I've never made the numbers work for musical revivals on the small scale – but it *is* possible to produce work.

Physical production budget

Physical production is all the elements of your design: set, costume, props, lighting, sound, transport, get-in, get-out, video (if required) and anything else on stage that isn't people, but might cost you money.

This is the trickiest section to budget as you do not have a design, designers, concept or anything concrete. So long as you're in the right ballpark to begin with, the designs can be governed by the budget, not the other way around. When money is tight, this is key. If you have a limited production budget, it will limit what your creative team are able to achieve, and potentially limit the creatives who will do the project. However, people make great work with small budgets *all the time*.

The production manager will manage this section of the budget. Ideally, you'll have them on board early enough to have their input as they should know what's realistic. However, usually the designers come before the production manager, and they'll want to know the rough budget before they sign up to the project, so it's on you.

Always remember you can tell a story around a kitchen table. Everything beyond that is a choice. There's almost always a clever creative solution to a problem, if discussed in enough time.

Set

Set can cost anything. One of my favourite designs for a show I've worked on cost £200 (it was always going to be my favourite, though, wasn't it?). Another cost £550. I've also spent £8000 on a set for a show in a tiny studio that I was general-managing. Generally speaking, realistic designs are more expensive to create than abstract. My two cheap designs made great use of builders' rubble and strip lights, and pallets, respectively.

Communication is key. Talk to your director about the budget limitations at the start. They can then have those conversations on day one with potential designers, and find ones that embrace the challenge. No one minds having a tiny budget if they know that to begin with (they'll not do the job if they do mind). They will mind *a lot* if their budget is reduced after they've started.

One mistake to avoid is to think that doing a show in the round will save you money because there's little set. It *will* save you money on the set. And you might green-light the show as a result. But you'll later discover you need four times the number of lights and speakers, and there's no shortcut. An expensive mistake. Yes, I am speaking from experience.

Costume

If it's a modern piece, this shouldn't cost too much, there are masses of second-hand modern clothes available cheaply. Period costumes are hard to fake, and probably require renting, which can be a significant cost. Again, consider abstract versus realism with your director. Could an Elizabethan comedy be a ruff (frilly Shakespearean neck warmer) combined with modern dress?

When reading a script and having initial conversations, beware suits (cheap suits look . . . cheap) and bespoke items that can't be fudged. I once spent more than 50 per cent of a costume budget on a baby bump for a pregnant character. Rentals are usually more expensive than purchases, but some costumes you just can't buy.

Also, don't forget to budget for laundry, particularly if it's a run with consecutive performances. Actors don't do their own. Some venues have laundry facilities, but most venues don't. Sending laundry out is time-consuming, expensive and logistically complicated. You may find it economical to buy multiple items of the same piece of costume to reduce laundry frequency – particularly if you're doing multiple performances a day. It is good (basically essential) practice to provide performers with a clean costume for every performance. Particularly shirts, underwear etc. It's a sweaty business. As a Swiss-Army-knife producer you could just do it at home every evening.

One trade-off when discussing costume is the need for a costume supervisor. This is someone to help the designer source all the bits of costume that they've designed. Unless your show is a two-hander where they're in one costume the whole time, sourcing costume is a time-consuming task. Costume supervisors are valuable but another drain on the budget. Could you do it? Could your designer simplify the designs? Or is there another solution? Probably you need a supervisor.

Props

Your props budget will depend hugely on the type of show you're doing. You can work it out from the script – if a prop is mentioned, the director will *probably* want it. There are two types of props, non-consumables and consumables.

Non-consumables are things you acquire once, and can give back, or sell on at the end – a kitchen pan or an umbrella. These can be bought, rented or borrowed.

Consumable props are exactly that. Food, fake blood, anything that's destroyed. A vase being broken in the script multiplies your vase budget by the number of performances . . . Consumable props can be a budget killer.

Your stage manager will manage getting hold of the props, unless it's a huge job, in which case you may need a specialist. I didn't work with a props supervisor until I was on a £300k show, so it's unlikely. Stage management are amazing.

In terms of budgeting, draw up a list, and do some research.

Lighting

Lighting budgets come down to how well stocked the venue is, and how accommodating your designer is. The main lighting cost is hiring lights. If the venue has all of the lights the designer requires, then there's almost no cost to you. When you get your venue's technical specifications (before you've signed the venue contract), find someone who understands lighting and ask them for help. If you're employing a decent designer, they're likely going to want some additional tools with which to design. Again, if you can't afford to hire, and the venue has a stock, find someone who'll make the best of it.

The only costs other than the lights themselves are gels (that turn lights different colours) and any 'practicals', which are lights built into the set. The total for all of these raw materials shouldn't be a significant cost in the context of the rest of the budget. If there are practicals in the design, you may need labour to build them into the set. Talk to your lighting designer.

Your creative team are doing your show in part to build up their portfolio. They will be looking to show off. Be clear when you contract them about the constraints of the budget/venue and you should be ok. I once used a West End lighting designer on an Off-West End show (he did it as a favour to the director). At an early production meeting he said he had everything he needed in the house stock, as the show wasn't about his lighting. I almost fell off my chair.

Sound

Sound designers are often self-deprecating about being left to the last. They usually have the least expectations on budget, and are able to do the most with the least.

Things to be aware of:

- Your venue may have just two speakers. This is enough for sound pointing in one direction from the centre of the space.
- Location-specific sound effects need a separate speaker.
- You will need to pay for the right to use any music played within the show that isn't composed specifically for the show (which you'll pay for separately). Talk to your venue about this; they may already have agreements you can use. In the UK this is done through an organization called PRS.
- You will likely require a laptop that is configured for Qlab – a programme all sound designers use to operate the sound. A Qlab license is also required.

As you can see, sound can also eat up budget. When you get the venue agreement, do they have a computer to operate the sound? Do they have

Qlab? How many speakers? Talk to your director, or designer if you have one.

Video

If you want projection in your show, you'll need to pay someone to design it. You'll need to hire a projector, you'll need to have someone technical in the venue every night who understands how it works. This may be a luxury beyond your budget ... but the same principles apply. It can usually be operated from Qlab along with your sound, so that's something!

Transport and miscellaneous

Even if you manage to get everything donated or borrowed for free, you're still going to need to get it to the venue. You'll need a van, parking fees, petrol etc.

On tour this is a significant expense. How small a vehicle can you fit everything in? How are the company travelling? Who's driving the van?

And miscellaneous is exactly that! Printing, buying costume rails etc. I'd suggest something similar to your props budget. Nothing too big, you'll have a separate contingency.

Theatre expenses

The most expensive cost is the theatre hire. Once you've done the deal it is fixed and completely unavoidable. Silver lining – it makes budgeting pretty easy. If it's a rental, then you should include it here. If it's a box office split, we'll deal with it in the income section and you can leave this blank.

How do you know what the rental would be? Some venues list it on their website. Get in touch with ones you'd like to work in and ask. You can negotiate on it later. Similar venues in a similar market are likely to be similar price. So, you can use one to estimate others until you get an accurate quote.

Auditions and rehearsals

You should be able to find somewhere to hold auditions cheaply – the best bet is to find a time when your venue is empty as they're most likely to give you a couple of days for free. If you don't have a casting director, you'll need a casting software subscription, (Spotlight, Backstage etc.), to find and communicate with potential performers. You can get the current cost from the website.

A rehearsal room can be a significant cost. It's a good area for scrappy cost-saving, though. The best way to budget is to look up rehearsal rooms and see what they charge. Then ring them up and ask if they offer discounts for emerging companies. Some spaces, particularly the bigger ones, can offer significant savings to the right people.

Fundamentally, anywhere is fine as long as your team are happy. Talk to your director. They are more likely to want the money spent on the set than on the rehearsal room.

Worth having a small amount in here for miscellaneous rehearsal room stuff – fruit, coffee, tea, folders, stationery etc. Little things that make the room a nicer place to work.

Press and marketing

There is so much to say about this. As you will soon find out. For now, however, we are just budgeting.

I tend to just pick a number. It sounds ridiculous, but you will spend every penny that you allocate here, so it's impossible to budget for need. You need to spend £50k. Doesn't mean you can!

Aim for 5 per cent to 15 per cent of your total budget. It's the only area of your budget that's helping you bring in audience, so it's key that it exists.

Administration

This is for all the other stuff. Insurance is essential – ring a company and ask for a quote. Legal . . . hopefully you won't need it. Accountancy, again – you can do the books yourself, it's not too complex. You must get professional advice about the legal and accountancy side around your business (as opposed to the show). More on all this administration in Part II – 'Making it happen'.

Opening night expenses feels like the first line that should go on a tight budget. However, after all the work that goes into the show, you have to write people a card and buy them a drink. At the very least. If you do delete it from the budget, expect to be paying for it out of your pocket. Or maybe find a bar or restaurant to cover it in return for some coverage in the programme?

Travel and accommodation

If you're touring, you're going to need to pay for your company to get around and for their accommodation. There are 'touring allowance' guidelines for weekly touring, but it's barely enough. My suggestion, go online and imagine you're a company member, how are they going to travel, how much is it going to cost and similarly for accommodation.

Producer fee

You've worked, you should be paid. Something in line with what you've paid the director is fair in a tight budget. You'll put in more time than anyone, but then you stand to gain the most. The vast majority of producers are the last to be paid. It's not great. Small-scale theatre producing is not how you're going to make a living, unfortunately.

Contingency

I keep a larger contingency than many producers. The extra cost makes it harder to make the budget work, but means I usually come in under-budget, as I have flexibility when problems arise.

I recommend using 10 per cent of the whole budget as contingency. This is pretty large, as many of the costs are fixed (the theatre, how much you're paying the cast, etc.). However, there's always something. It's great to be able to solve a key problem with money if you have to at the crunch.

Understand this, however. Your production manager and design team will *expect* you to have a contingency. They will spend all of their budget on day one (because it's not big enough) and plead ignorance when all the little extras come in later. However hard I've tried, I've never managed to bring a production budget in at the budget I told them they had. Some designers (and production managers) will expect the contingency, so you need a bigger contingency than they realize to cover for any *actually* unexpected costs.

I've been known to budget for something I suspect we'll never need, acting as a second contingency that even I forget about. I'm sure other people manage it more closely and accurately – this is the method that works for me.

If you're not VAT-registered, then your contingency also covers the possibility of a VAT-registered actor. It's a killer when you first come across one, but legally they have to add VAT to their invoice, and you can't claim it back if you're not registered. Most actors aren't VAT-registered, so we don't budget for it, but it's the sort of possibility the contingency is for.

Royalties

As we've already touched on, royalties are how you will pay your writer. They are calculated as a percentage of net box office. As I mentioned earlier, you should expect to pay a new writer 4 per cent to 6 per cent, and if you manage to get an Arthur Miller play, it's likely to be 10 per cent minimum. These are *always* negotiable. Whatever the big scary agent says. Explain your project, your budget and your costs, and be prepared to walk away. You'll be surprised.

The advance that you pay the writers when you sign the deal, does not need to sit in the budget as a cost, as it's recoupable (you will take all of the royalty income up until the point you have 'recouped' their advance). However, you do need to add it to the amount of money you have to raise.

Income

Income comes from a number of sources. To begin with we're just going to look at box office.

We need to work out what the total net box office (NBO) is, if you sold every ticket, and then work out how much you'd make if you sold smaller percentages of that figure. Based on this theoretical calculation of the number of tickets you need to sell, you can tell whether the show is commercially viable, or whether you're going to need subsidy.

To get your net box office, take the number of performances, multiply by number of seats, multiplied by average ticket price to get your total possible income (known as gross box office). From here, take off credit card fees (budget 4 percent, get the real amount from your venue agreement) and taxes, (VAT in the UK), and you have your total net box office.

For our income projections we then draw up a chart with different percentages of this.

Let's say a show's NBO was £10 000.

100 per cent NBO – £10 000

90 per cent NBO – £9 000

80 per cent NBO – £8 000

70 per cent NBO – £7 000

60 per cent NBO – £6 000

50 per cent NBO – £5 000

40 per cent NBO – £4 000

30 per cent NBO – £3 000, etc.

Compare these numbers to your expenditure. How does it look?

If you need to sell 50 per cent of tickets or below, then you likely have a commercially viable show (presuming a realistic venue capacity). This is a great situation as it leaves open all the methods of raising money.

More likely, you'll need to sell more than 50 per cent of your tickets to break even. Possibly even more than 100 per cent of tickets. Don't despair, there are options. The majority of small shows fall into this category. You're going to need to find subsidy to make it viable.

West End terminology

Unsurprisingly, larger-scale budgets are more complicated. I want to help clarify some terms you may hear and why they're less relevant on the smaller scale. If they mean nothing to you, that's no problem!

- Venue contra – larger venues split up their hire into 'rent' and 'contra'. A contra is the actual cost of running the venue. The rent is on top of that. It's highly likely that your venue costs are completely fixed.

- Pre-production versus running costs – bigger budgets are split into costs before you start performances (the pre-production), and repeated weekly costs after opening (running costs). As venues pay out box office on a Friday for the previous week, you can use this weekly ticket income to pay your bills for the following week, therefore reducing the amount of money you need upfront.

  Smaller venues pay out the box office three to four weeks after the production closes, so you need to have paid all your 'running costs' before you have a penny of income, so this distinction is (almost) irrelevant. One exception is if you manage to make tax relief work – more below.

- Weeks to recoupment – this is a measure that comes from shows that have no fixed length of run, and means, 'How many weeks of performances until this show recoups it's upfront costs'. Again, probably of no relevance to you!

- Post-recoupment royalty – some rights contracts will increase the writer's royalty after the producer has recouped their investment. It's a commercial theatre clause I would avoid. Defining the point at which you've recouped on a fixed-length short run is complicated.

- Royalty pool – a complicated royalty structure alternative, largely for big musicals. Not used at this scale.

Theatre tax relief

Theatre tax relief (TTR) exists in the UK to incentivize the making of theatre. While called a tax relief, in reality it works more like a cash rebate against costs of production.

At the end of a production, you are entitled to ask the government to reimburse you for a percentage of your pre-production costs outside of press and marketing. The level of this percentage changes, but will be available on a government website. Typically, it means that three to six months after the show has ended, it's possible to get a payout from the government for 5 per cent to 10 per cent of your total costs.

This should be fantastic for smaller theatre and for budgeting. However, in order to do this, you need to pay an accountant. In the past I've been quoted more for an accountant than I was due back in TTR.

It is possible. Find a tame accountant to do it for less or have your business accountant include it as part of the end-of-year accounts. Definitely investigate, as it can be a great bonus for the show.

What to do if it doesn't add up?

Ok. You have the most detailed budget you can manage. You've put in place your income table, and you look at it. And it doesn't add up. It never adds up first time around. What do you do?

All of the below are options. Not all of them do I recommend.

- Cut the budget. If you have a director, bring them into this process. Can you do a week's less rehearsal? Could they manage without a stage manager at the beginning of rehearsals? Is there room in the set budget for simplification? All of the costs have an artistic compromise attached to them – the question is what you're willing to forego. A single chair in the middle of the stage might be all the set you need. If there're no sounds you don't need a sound designer. Wouldn't the show look good under strip light?!

  Try to preserve the marketing and press budget. That is money that helps bring in box office. Everything else is a sunk cost, but those costs work for you.

  Do at this point try to renegotiate the venue and royalties. If the show is currently not viable, you have nothing to lose.

- Increase the income. This is the easiest way to make the budget work on paper. However, increasing the number of performances only increases the number of people who are going to have to buy a ticket. Ten per cent of a 1,000-seat house is a full 100-seat house, even if the budgets look completely different. I once ran a show for five weeks rather than the normal four because it looked better on paper. Ultimately it only increased the risk and the amount of money the show lost.

Increasing the ticket price is the other way to do this, and is something to consider, within reason. You can always bring the price down later through discounting. Many venues have fixed pricing, which may rule this out.

- Raise 'soft' money that you don't have to give back. Grants, sponsorship or private donations. It's how a vast amount of theatre is made.

Be careful. We can all say 'I'll get the money from the Arts Council', but what happens if you don't? First-time applications are hard, and should not be relied on, unless you can hold off on signing the venue deal until you have a decision – but more on that later. When considering subsidy, always work out your backup plan.

- Choose a different venue. This may sound odd but is more sensible than you might think. Other venues might have a higher average capacity. They might be cheaper, or they might command a higher ticket price. No one is stopping you from talking to multiple venues and running multiple budgets.

- Choose a new show. Fewer actors. Simpler design. Lower royalties. If you're the writer, write a smaller one! Why do you think so many shows at fringe festivals are one-person shows, with the writer as the performer?

- Talk to your team. I once booked a tour for a successful show but was only able to get a couple of performances per location rather than the full week I'd budgeted. I booked lots of fantastic venues where the show would have been great, but based on my budgeting, I didn't get enough of them.

As a result of this, I pulled the tour. That may have been the right decision, but I wish I'd spoken to the team, presented what I'd done and seen if they were interested in making it work. It could have worked on a day rate per performance, and if they were happy, it could've gone out. I've always regretted not having the conversation.

Summary

Budgeting is a vital process to go through. Everything starts with the budget. Once the budget is in good shape the whole project starts to come together.

- Budgeting is key. Start as soon as you can.
- Keep adjusting your budget as you get more information to make it as accurate as possible.

- Preserve your marketing budget wherever possible.
- Don't overstate the realistic income. Fifty per cent capacity is *high*.
- If the first budget doesn't add up, keep going! It will eventually.
- Don't sign the venue deal until you've made it add up.

You've got a budget, and you know what money you need. Now you can start to look at how to raise the money.

INTERVIEW WITH RACHEL DANIELS (PART 2)

I wanted to include this short exchange with Rachel that is more relevant to budgeting than choosing a script – relating to the discussions around smaller-scale, lesser-paid work. I don't think we'll ever completely agree, but it's an indication of the world you're entering into!

Tim Johanson   You said that on the small-scale creatives are subsidizing a production. I would agree. Do you think that's exclusively a bad thing?

Rachel Daniels   I do think it's bad because they get exploited and really badly.

TJ   In terms of?

RD   Fee paid in relation to hours.

TJ   But to expand on that, bearing in mind I'm fully against profit share, if creatives were always paid at union rates, we would not have 50 per cent of the theatres in London. They just wouldn't exist.

RD   I don't know what the answer is. All I know is that I struggle to see how you can justify the level of fees that people are being asked to accept. And they do accept, because it's a piece that they passionate about and therefore, they really want to do it and it might help their career. And that's what the producer is saying. And *then* it's a new musical and they only get two and a half weeks rehearsal. And . . . I could go on.

TJ   I don't know what the answer is either. Do you think producers are exploiting them because the producers are financially benefiting from it?

RD   No, I don't necessarily think that. It comes from the point where the venue is saying, this is what our rental is, because we only have this many seats. I'm not a producer and I'm probably not best placed to have an answer for it, but there's something wrong in the economics.

TJ   I was interested in the word 'exploits', I guess, because exploit implies to me, somebody else is benefiting.

RD   I don't know. A producer in order to survive has to be commercially minded. And therefore, I suspect there is a level of exploitation because the producer, understandably, is trying to maximise their profit. And the only way of doing that is by minimising their budget. And they're being squeezed from both ends by the venue and by the agents of the creatives. And they've somehow got to extract profit out of that situation, but it doesn't work. It doesn't work for all those individuals who are contributing to those productions.

TJ   You don't think they get benefit out of it?

RD   They might do, but they're not earning a living.

TJ   My argument would be, neither is the producer at this scale, everyone's just trying to make work.

5

Raising the money

Whether it's £1k, or £100k, the first amount of money you'll have to raise is going to feel big. It did for me. These are sums of money that you probably don't deal with in your day-to-day life.

Don't worry. Approach it logically, do your preparation, be confident in your numbers and be secure that if you can't raise it, you can make appropriate adjustments, or can call it off.

Having drawn up your budget you know how much money you need, and therefore whether you have a commercially viable project, or whether it will require subsidy. Or whether you're going to have to find a clever way of combining the two.

Then you have to crack on and do it. You will never find out if you can do it until you try. I have raised money for both commercial and subsidized projects. They require the same thing, clear reasons for doing the show (whatever they are), a competent plan for delivering the show and clear budgeting. And passion. Always passion.

Generally speaking, you have to choose either a commercial or a subsidized route. The bodies that provide subsidy will not allow that subsidy to be used to help other people make profit. Which makes sense. As such we're going to look at them as separate entities before looking at some blended situations that satisfy all parties.

Commercial

Raising commercial investment is simple conceptually. You raise money as investment in the show, with a view to returning a profit, but with the possibility of making a loss. That's it.

In its most basic terms, you ask people for money to pay for your show. You spend their money getting your show on. Then you split the box office with them in a prearranged manner. Investors take any money left over after all your costs up to the point where they have all their money back.

After that it is a profitable show – a hit. At this stage all profits are split between the investor and the producer. In the UK this is usually 60:40 in the investor's favour; in the United States, it's 50:50. Random though it may look, this is a standard agreement that has been around for decades and serves commercial theatre well.

This investment is somewhere between a loan and a conventional company investment. It's not a case of selling shares in your business like most investments. It's a bespoke arrangement.

All investments, in the UK at least, are regulated by the Financial Conduct Authority. To avoid the costs associated with this, the theatre industry operates a system that people can self-certify that they are either a high net-worth individual, or a sophisticated investor.

As ever, seek advice from existing producers and people who've been there before.

Approaching investors

My tips on raising commercial money:

- Make a list of every person you have a connection to who invests in anything. That's your potential investor list.
- Delete from that list anyone who can't say no. Parents etc. For me the guilt of losing their money would be too great.
- From there, shift your mindset. If your project is *truly* commercial, you're offering them an opportunity. It's not charity. If you had the money, you'd want to invest it all yourself, because it's an *opportunity*. Set up a chat, ask if investing in theatre was something they'd consider. If not, no worries. If yes, then sell your opportunity.
- If someone wants to co-produce with you, and they're willing to raise a significant portion of the money, don't be precious about titles. Calling someone a co-producer costs you nothing.

Putting together a commercial package at the smaller scale is possible, but it's not easy, and it usually requires a famous actor.

So, what do most people do?

Subsidized/not-for-profit

Most art does not make money. Almost all of it, in fact. Visual art, opera, ballet – none of these operate commercially, they are all subsidized in one form or another. They are funded by the government, trusts and foundations, local councils, corporations and private donations. All of these options are available to you but none happen quickly. So, crack on! And don't sign the venue deal yet.

Grant-making bodies

Grants for making art are made by both local and national government bodies, and private trusts and foundations.

They all have an application process, and guidelines as to what they are and aren't able to fund. They all have a focus or agenda, and the best place to start is researching them on their website. You can then decide if your project is appropriate, reach out to them for advice and apply. Be conscious of their application dates, and decision-making timelines. Projects funded by grants need to be planned a long way out.

Arts Council

We are fortunate in the UK to have the Arts Council, the government's outlet for funding the arts. Most European countries have something similar. I've successfully worked only with Arts Council England (ACE), but Creative Scotland and the Arts Councils of Wales and Northern Ireland are similar. I'll refer to ACE processes for now.

There are a series of funds that ACE uses to distribute funds. The main one relevant to getting a show on is (currently) called the Project Grants fund. It used to be called Grants for the Arts. By the time you're reading this ... who knows!

Like all funding bodies ACE has an agenda. Spend considerable time getting your head around what their current agenda is, and work out how your project fits into it. Then look at the application form and what they're assessing against.

The application process changes relatively regularly. Through my time engaging with the fund, they have always cared about:

- How the work fits their strategy/goals.
- How accurately it's budgeted, and how much other supporting funding you've generated.
- Whether you're paying everyone involved appropriately.
- What other partners are involved, and the credibility they bring to the piece.
- Who is going to manage the project to ensure it gets delivered.

- How by receiving the grant, it is going to transform the project and your career.
- Who, where and when are people going to consume the art – and where the audience is.

Try to talk to a relationship manager about your project. They know the system best and can guide you through it. Start with the main advice line, and see how you go. If you don't get anywhere, try to find some names and write directly. If you're polite, the worst they can say is that they're too busy. An introduction from someone who knows somebody is obviously best.

These grants are particularly great for funding research and development, using ACE money to develop new work through a workshop and with an industry presentation. You can apply for funding without specific venue dates, so if you don't get the grant, you're not committed to a venue.

Other trusts and foundations

There are other trusts and foundations out there that fund the arts. They all have different eligibilities and application processes. Many reject non-charities, but some are happy to hear from individuals or even companies where the project is not-for-profit. Again, you must apply with enough time; these can take a long time to come through. I know of fringe shows that have received money from three or four different foundations. It's labour-intensive, but a really good idea. Do your research and apply.

Crowdfunding

There's loads written about crowdfunding. It's a fantastic way to raise funds for something without a specific start date (a film or a product prototype); however, it's a tricky way to raise money for theatre. The hook with crowdfunding is the project will happen only *when* it's fully funded. However, the majority of theatre crowdfunding happens once the project is green-lit already, so there's no specific urgency for someone to donate, they know you're going to do the show anyway.

If you want it to be effective, then you need to get a venue agreed in principle, and an 'I need to raise £X by Y date, to make the project happen' message. Having the show on sale will undercut that message.

It can be a useful marketing tool additionally, as it gives you an excuse to start talking about the show. If you create a message with a real 'need' and attract 50–100 donors, all those people are going to be seriously engaged when you make it happen for real.

You will have to make a compelling pitch, have a realistic target and be persistent. But if you get it, it's great. It's unrestricted funds towards your show (and can help a lot with the 'other income' for your Arts Council application).

Crowdfunding fatigue is real. Your friends and family may help once, even twice, but beyond that it becomes tiresome. So pick the right project.

Private donations

Lots of theatre happens because someone knows someone who is willing to lose money on it. This happens at all scales of theatre. There is just not enough Arts Council funding to go around. Don't underestimate this as a source of funds, even if your immediate network is not well-off.

Having a wealthy 'angel' who wants to see you succeed is the quickest and cleanest way to funding your show. I have never found one of these, but I know they exist. I've seen shows funded by someone's relatives, someone involved in the show or, indeed, someone who just met someone who wants to be supportive. Good luck to you if this is you, but please don't worry/ despair if it's not!

A charity I used to work for wrote to people in the public eye who might have some spare cash they'd be willing to share for the right project. These approaches consisted of a polite letter addressed to them, via their agent, explaining specifically why we were writing to them and thought they might find our project worthwhile. At worst, you will be ignored or receive a polite rejection, and you might end up with some remarkable keepsake letters from the process!

Sponsorship

Sponsorship has always seemed to me like a better idea in principle than in practice. In principle you get a business to sponsor the show, in return for a presence in the programme, on the website and potentially on the marketing. Big shows do it, and if you can manage it, it's money you don't have to return.

At the smaller scale, it's hard to justify this to a business on purely commercial terms, as the reach you're able to offer just isn't large enough. Where I have seen it succeed, it has come through a personal connection. My guess is their motivation then has been more 'outreach in the arts' than 'opportunity to grow our brand'.

If you can make the right connection, you can offer to distribute their logo on your materials, organize a night for their staff to watch, have a drink with the cast afterwards, or whatever else they might be interested in. Getting that connection is the key.

Do think about smaller-scale opportunities. A local wine shop might save you a bill for wine on opening night in return for being on the website, or a printing shop might do you a deal in return for your promoting them. There's no wrong answer here, this is about being an entrepreneur and thinking about where you might be able to save money.

Combination fundraising

So, there are purely subsidized and purely commercial ways to raise money. Grant-making bodies rightly make it difficult to combine the two. But we're making small-scale work. At this level we're all hustlers. You need to raise the money, however you can. There are more options.

- Commercial with elements of subsidized

  Raise most of the money commercially, but go after sponsorship in a big way. Or, is there someone you know who really wants to support you or the show, and would be willing to be a donor, while others are investing? They could give their money as 'last out' investment, so everyone else gets theirs back first. Or just give it as a gift. Both would make the budget more commercially viable.

  A key show in my career incorporated both of those, £10k as a gift and £5k as a last out investment. It was all organized in advance and everyone got what they wanted out of it. The show wouldn't have happened without it.

  Perhaps a crowdfunder designed to make your show commercially viable? Could you promote your crowdfunder with a message 'I need £5k donated in order to unlock the remaining £20k investment in my show'? Only you can know if you'd be comfortable with that message, but I don't see any reason it shouldn't work.

- Subsidized with elements of commercial

  'Payback'

  This relies on embracing the idea that there are people who might 'invest' with you, who have no expectation of seeing their money again. If you raise subsidy from trusts and foundations, the rules are that you can't pay profit to investors. Fair enough. But you should be able to return a loan (depending on the rules of the trust/foundation you've raised from). If someone wants to support you, it's rare that they're actually looking to make money. Just promise to spend any leftover funds on the next show!

  'Bad commercial'

  You don't have the funding restrictions of the 'Payback' model, but your show is highly unlikely to pay profit. If you have people who want to invest with you, they are unlikely to want to make money. Explain the situation, and see if they will invest on a 'bad commercial' model. You'll pay back whatever you can. Most likely, they'll lose some or all of their money, but if it happens to take off, they can have some profit as well.

- Co-productions

  If you manage to secure a co-production with a producing house, fantastic. There are three models here. With all of them you should expect to pay a royalty to the producing house when you're presenting the show.

  - You split both the costs and the box office at the co-production house.
  - They pay for it all, and keep all the box office – but you get to produce it afterwards.
  - You give them a contribution, they make it and keep all the box office. You get the show cheaper than if you had produced it yourself. This is called 'enhancing' a production and is the model many larger shows use.

  This allows you to raise your money whichever method you like, and as long as you do a good deal, you will get a cheaper show – as if you'd raised subsidy. Plus all the other advantages to working with an established producing house.

Subsidized cash flow problems

One of the downsides to funding a show through subsidy is cash flow. You are going to include an estimate of box office in any funding application. Forty per cent of your budget, say, will come from box office. The problem is that you won't receive any of that box office from the venue until four weeks after you close, and 100 per cent of your costs have been spent. Grant bodies also hold back a percentage of their money until after you have evaluated the entire project. These combined can leave you 40 to 50 per cent down on the cash you need.

What are your options? Well, hopefully your venue is taking its rent out of the box office, which will help. Are there some invoices you could delay paying until box office comes through? Big lighting or sound companies might allow this. And I don't know a producer who takes their fee until *way* after the end of the show. It's all a bit of a fudge.

If your show is doing well, and is taking box office that is considerably more than the venue rent, the venue might consent to giving an early payout halfway through a run. Even Edinburgh venues will do this if you ask them nicely. If your show is struggling, this is less likely. Venues will take what's due to them first.

Backup plans – what do I do if I don't get any funding but have signed a theatre?

It is highly unadvisable to find yourself in this position. Theatre production is a juggling act and ideally you will have all your money before you sign a theatre. This is not always possible – but bear in mind that if you sign the venue deal, you will be liable for the full rental period. Make sure you have some emergency plan if the funding doesn't come through. Crudely, this is likely to be you, or someone you know. Get the funding first, and you won't have to worry about it.

If you *can* cover the shortfall, then feel free to crack on with the show, you can carry on raising money until opening night. Just know what the worst-case scenario is.

Summary

I imagine that this is the part that you find the most daunting. I certainly did. I know of people who've spent years not producing because they worry about raising the money. The only way you can find out if you can raise the money is by trying.

If you approach it the right way . . . it can be fun. Really. Talking to people about your passion is fun. Certainly, as you raise it bit by bit, you'll feel a huge sense of achievement.

But don't hang around. You should be thinking about how you can raise money from the minute you start thinking about a project. And you must know where the money is coming from before you green-light a show. Or else disaster lies ahead.

Write your budget, make a plan and crack on. If you're clear and honest, you'll be amazed what you can do.

- Do you have a commercially viable show? If so, all options are open.
- If not, where is the subsidy going to come from? Explore crowdfunding, chat to an Arts Council relationship manager, work out if you have contacts who'd like to support you.
- Get started!
- Hustle. It's all a hustle. Keep going.
- Don't sign the venue deal until you have the money, or can personally cover the shortfall.

INTERVIEW WITH PAULA VARJACK, ARTS COUNCIL ENGLAND RELATIONSHIP MANAGER

Paula is a successful interdisciplinary artist, who also happens to be an Arts Council England Relationship Manager. I was delighted to interview Paula as she has huge experience on both sides of the funding application process.

Tim Johanson   Can you tell me a bit about your background?

Paula Varjack   I've had lots of different careers. I originally had no interest in being a performer, I trained in stage management and technical production at RADA.

After a final module there in television production, I then went on to film school. I specialized in producing and screenwriting, and gained a lot of foundational ideas about producing, but was left with no idea as to how to get a job in the industry. So I ended up working in retail and bartending, making short films on the side.

Eventually I ended up working for a global animation company looking after audio production – voice records, castings, music production and mixes. I did that for a few years. I got really frustrated with what we were making and the lack of progression in the role. I left and went to Berlin on a six-month 'break' to finish editing a film.

I knew few people. I was open to everything and fell into performance. And then from that point it was, it was all I wanted to do. I blagged my way into various performance scenes (spoken word, experimental performance, queer cabaret) and miraculously made a career I could live from. I came back to London to retrain in performance. And since then, I've been a theatre maker and interdisciplinary artist.

TJ   Have producing and making work always been interconnected for you?

PV   Producing has run through what I'm doing from the outset and predates me being a creative in the way that I am now. Often for example, writing an application is the way I find myself into making a new work. So even though I find it frustrating (I mean I don't 'enjoy' application writing), by the end of the application, I have a much clearer idea of what the project is that I'm trying to make.

I always encourage artists to at least familiarize themselves with the bid writing process. Because even if you want to get someone else in to do it, it's good to know what it is you are asking for. And genuinely, it's good to have your own know-how about how to put together your own projects.

TJ   I couldn't agree more. The premise of this book is allowing people to be able to take control of what they're trying to achieve.

PV   And understand what other people are asking of you too. Right? So if you get a contract, or you're given a fee, or there's something re. budgets, that you have some sort of sense of the narrative, whether you make sense in it, and what questions you should be asking.

TJ   Tell me about what a relationship manager does?

PV   The key to the title is that you manage relationships with a number of organizations that are part of the national portfolio, the core funded organizations. You're somewhere in between critical friends on behalf of the Arts Council, looking after the investment, but also are a conduit for that organization back to the Arts Council, sharing information and keeping aware of opportunities that might be relevant for them.

     You will also be on panels reviewing Project Grants. There are two relationship managers on panels for the lower threshold grants (currently under £30k). One acts as Chair. And – they can be from *any* artform . . . (which is the thing that definitely blew my mind when I started).

TJ   So, you could have an application for one thing reviewed by other specialties?

PV   You could have a theatre application reviewed by a visual arts relationship manager and a museums relationship manager. If something was craft specific, then they would reach out to someone in that team. But surprisingly, even if it's not your discipline, you can still pick through the narrative, because it's telling a story of a project effectively, and giving you the information you need in order for you to make sense of it.

     So as an applicant you need to find a way (in the limited character count!) to be engaging and have your energy come through, while definitely answering all the questions. It's definitely not easy, but it's possible.

     Back when I very first began applying for grants, I always got my father to look over my applications, explicitly because I thought, 'Well, if someone who was outside of the arts understands what I've written, it'll definitely be clear to whoever reads it'. And I've since discovered, that was really good advice that I stumbled on for myself. But essentially anyone you can get to read over it who's outside the project is going to be a big help.

     Relationship managers also do advisory sessions. So, for example, maybe someone is applying for the first time, and anyone anywhere can reach out to customer services for advice and they can be really helpful – especially around some of the more technical aspects of the application.

At the moment we're prioritizing first time applicants, then people who have protected characteristics who have been historically underrepresented within funding. Also, if you've been unsuccessful with an application, you can ask for an advisory session to look at the application.

TJ So, first time applicants should call up customer service.

PV They can. And they can ask about local advice sessions – sometimes these might be group sessions. Personally, I think you will get far more out of it if you apply and then if you're unsuccessful, ask for the session. Because once you've had it, then you may be unlikely to be offered another one.

TJ What's the best piece of advice you can give someone applying to the Arts Council for the first time?

PV The first place you should always start with is the ACE website, because that will give the most up-to-date information about the guidelines. For example, the current Project Grants is within the framework of Let's Create, our 10-year strategy. The best thing you could do to start with, is become really familiar with that strategy.

Effectively any funder has some kind of agenda, whether it's corporate or nonprofit, there's some, either values or ideology that they want to promote or support. Let's Create is ACE's strategy. So you need to tell a story that your project is aligned with their strategy.

Maybe it's about the fact that you are a first-time maker and you are developing a practice in a certain way, and this project is going to take you to this whole other level. Maybe what you're doing is innovative for the artform in itself. Maybe you're working with exciting community groups that you have relationships with – but ideally you should see something in that strategy that's connected with what you want to do too. And then it's telling that story of – *we're both on the same page.* That would be my absolutely number one piece of advice.

The other thing I often hear is, start with the budget. It's not how I start, but it's how one of my collaborators often starts.

It's a good place to begin because you can start to see what is the timeline you're thinking of, who are the kind of people you want to work with, what partners you might need to reach out for.

You know, it's also a really daunting thing just to start planning, right? So making a budget before you start to get excited about the ideas and tell the story of the project, there is an inherent story in those budget lines as well.

Doing a project plan, even if it's vague, right from the beginning of your planning is a good idea too. Like if you know that you're going to be presenting this work at a venue in a particular season – it's part of a festival and you want it to be in that etc., you can work back from those dates

But also, always in that timeline allow for resubmission time. I always make the assumption I'm not going to be successful the first time I apply even if I feel I have the strongest possible application.

On that day when your project is assessed by the panel, so many things need to be aligned. There are inevitably always more fundable and exciting applications than there is money for. It just is how it is. And there's a whole number of criteria that needs to be balanced within that, in terms of art form, in terms of people at different stages of their career, in terms of geographical spread, thematic issues and so on. And you have no idea who you're going to be up against. So you should build in that you might not be successful the first time.

And if you're not successful and the feedback suggests you have a strong application, then it's about making small changes and putting it back in. And if the feedback suggests your application was weak in certain areas, at the very least you have some feedback about what are the areas that you need to tweak before you put it back in.

The first time I ever applied, I was unsuccessful. One of the things I was told by artist friends when I applied was, 'Don't submit when it's clear that the dates mean you need to get the funding and then the activity starts the next day'. And I was like, 'That doesn't make sense to me. I know that I need it! And I've already got this opportunity, so I'm just going to apply'.

But now that makes sense, because if it's that tight, you're telling the story that you're going to do it anyway. And you need to make a case that if it wasn't for this funding, this project cannot go ahead in the way you would want it to. If you're on a project that will go ahead no matter what, and someone else is telling the story that without this funding, the project is over. It's not as high stakes for you.

And if it *is* the case that without the funding the project can't happen, that has to be explicit within the application. 'I've got all these partners on board. But if I do not get this funding, then I will not be able to take advantage of these opportunities that are furthering my practice'.

TJ   Are you more likely to succeed if you ask for less money?

PV   It's a tricky one. You are the only person who knows how much your project costs. There has to be a narrative and it has to be something that you're able to clearly explain as to where those figures come from, because things cost what they cost.

It's not a good idea to under-budget. Both because it can show and also because ACE really cares about people being paid fairly.

It will cost what it costs. There has to be a clear logic for it. And you need to spell out that logic within your application, and then it needs to be cross-referenced with some kind of recognized structure, like rate guidance from a union.

Also, if you don't have any match funding, and that could be in kind support, then that makes it seem like you don't have investment, you don't have partnerships in place. It's not even necessarily about money, but it's showing that there's a demand for the work, it's showing that other people have a commitment to seeing this project happen. That makes for a stronger application too.

TJ   Yeah. Interesting.

PV   And the other top tip, when I'm writing applications, is to ask yourself, are you answering the questions? And that sounds silly, but especially as an artist, you get passionate and excited about your idea, sometimes you run away talking about that idea, but you're not actually answering the questions on the application. After you have a draft, go back and check your answers against the guidance – don't just read the guidance before you start the application – read it again when you've got a first draft.

And then finally the other thing is asking yourself *how* you're going to do something. So, if you say I'm going to reach this audience. Yeah. Great. How are you going to do it? How are you going to reach those people? What are the tools you're going to use? What is this based on? And who are your audience (or who do you imagine them to be).

Part I – Conclusion

Wow. You've found a great script. You've got the perfect venue. And amazingly you've raised the money. You are officially a producer. And a pretty good one at that. You've got further than most people.

Not so bad after all? Maybe a little bit fun? Hope so. You've got a heck of a way to go, but really, this *was* the hard bit. It's also the most important bit. If you choose a bad script, you're stuffed on day one. If you choose the wrong venue, your job is going to be a hassle from the off.

And if you kick off without having raised the money? I hope you have deep pockets or rich friends.

But you've smashed all three. You can sign the rights deal, the venue contract and get into the nitty-gritty of making it happen.

- Remember that the play's the thing. It's crucial that you love what you're producing.
- Don't panic if you don't have the money to pay for the rights upfront. There are options available.
- Make sure you've attended a show at your venue before you sign a deal if at all possible.
- You'll never know if you can raise the money unless you try.
- Don't sign the venue deal until you know where the money's coming from.
- This is producing as a juggling act. It's the same for everyone.

PART II

Making it happen

6

First steps to making it happen

You've found the show, obtained a license, signed a theatre and raised the money. Now you have to make it happen! This is the general management, the nuts and bolts of getting a show on.

You're going to appoint a creative and production team, go through the casting process and write a lot of contracts. You're going to manage the budget, the bookkeeping, rehearsals, the tech period and opening night. You're going to manage egos of all shapes and sizes and keep the show pointing in the right direction. And you're going to write a lot of lists.

This section is about general management.

What is a general manager?

The general manager is the most senior administrator on a show. They are in charge of appointing and contracting the team, managing the production budget and ensuring everyone is paid. Other duties might include liaising with the marketing and press team, organizing photo shoots and interviews or booking the rehearsal room. They are the first port of call for problems, and report to the producer everything that's going on.

We mentioned the distinction between general manager and producer in Chapter 1 because it's a key one. The likelihood is, if being the producer is your only role on the show, you will general-manage as well. It's an indulgence to pay someone separate.

If you have multiple roles, particularly if you're part of rehearsals, and your workload is going to be too much, bringing in a general manager is a great idea. Call them the producer if you like, pay them the producer fee, but don't forget, the title is a façade. You're in charge so *you* are the producer.

Don't expect them to make big decisions, or take responsibility for stuff that you should be responsible for.

Company set-up

It is a good idea to set up a company to produce shows of any significant scale. There are provisos in company law that protect individuals in the event of disaster, if a company is the producing entity. In British law companies are 'limited', meaning the liability if something goes wrong is limited to the assets of the company. Crucially, not your personal assets, as long as you act within the law.

You can be listed as the producer, but the legal entity, and name on all contracts should not be yours.

Say, you produce the show and something awful happens that costs a lot of money. And, say, your insurance company claim they don't cover it. And the venue claims it's not their responsibility. Somebody bigger and with deeper pockets than you could come after the producing entity for the costs.

As long as you have acted within the law and are producing through a company limited by shares they can only come after the company. Not the director of the company. Because the liability of the company is 'limited'.

I've been threatened with legal action twice on London fringe shows. Which is more than I expected when I started out! Neither time did the other side have a case, but there's no money to fight these things at that scale. In both cases the legal advice was to wait until we'd closed, because there was little money in the company, so there was little they could go after. If it had been produced in my name, they could have, theoretically, come after anything I personally owned. I love theatre, but I don't love it enough to risk my flat. And nor should you.

Who knows what the worst-case scenario is? But you should be confident that if you have acted legally, you are personally safe.

You're also going to need a business bank account. So set one up.

Company law

I'm not even going to try to explain company law here. But if you *do* set up a company (as you should), then you will be the director of the company, and therefore have obligations as a director of a company. Look them up, it's not a lot of effort over the year, but you are legally obliged to do them.

And if you're in the UK, learn what the annual return is. (Ok, it's now called the confirmation statement.) It's not the same thing as corporation taxes. And if you don't send it in, and somehow miss their reminders they'll shut down the company and take all of its assets. And you won't know it's happened. And you'll panic. And you'll get to know the people at Companies House really well on the phone. And you'll spend extra money on an accountant. And months later you might fix it and be able to return that money to the investors, whose money it actually was. And you will never, ever, forget again.

Learn what you have to do. I have. The wrong way.

VAT registration

As discussed in the venue deal, avoid VAT registration if you can. Keeping under the registration threshold (£85k at time of writing) could make 5 to 10 per cent difference to your bottom line. So long as you've worked out how the venue's attitude to VAT works.

You can register retrospectively. If you are expecting to take £50k on a show, and end up taking £100k, you can register after the fact. You can also apply for an exemption from registering, if it's likely to be a temporary rise over the VAT threshold, which on a limited run show it almost certainly will be (once you close, you'll go back to taking nothing each month). I've done this successfully and it turned a 95 per cent return to investors to a 105 per cent return, which was satisfying.

If you do register, you have to send in a VAT return every quarter. And you *probably* need an accountant to do that for you. Another reason to avoid it.

Be aware that your team will expect you to be VAT-registered. It's customary for them to budget using net figures. Builders, costume makers, everyone will quote net of VAT. If you are not going to be registered, you must make absolutely clear to your team that their budget is a gross figure. You're probably going to need to mention this at budget stage, at design stage, at the first production meeting, at the second production meeting, at the third production meeting . . .

Summary

Lots of people can help with this. It's the same outside of the theatre industry. Take advice and get it right. It doesn't take very long to found a company (it's remarkably quick), and is essential moving forward.

- Understand what a general manager is and how they can help.
- Set up a company to be the producer.
- Do know your company law. It's, quite literally, the law.

Now, on to the fun bits.

7

Appointing the creative and production teams

It requires a diverse range of skills to put on any piece of theatre. This range of skills is barely different in a fifty-seat studio than at the London Palladium. You don't have them. Your director doesn't have them. You need a team.

The difference between the West End and the small studio is money. All theatre is run a little on goodwill, but the smaller the scale the more important it becomes.

You need three distinct groups of people, creatives, production team and actors. Creatives are primarily your director and designers, but might include a choreographer, fight director or video designer.

The production manager, the most important appointment you will make, heads up your production team. It then includes the stage management, and any other technicians needed.

Actors are getting their own chapter later. For now, it's the creative and production team.

Representation

Theatre, like society, has historically been the preserve of the privileged. And, bluntly, continues to be. It's vital that those in the positions of power do everything they can to address this. By becoming a producer, you are becoming one of those people in power.

As a person who holds a veritable royal flush of privilege, I am the last person to lecture on how to do this. I am continually trying to get better at it. It would be great if this issue was 'solved' in the next decade, but I suspect we'll all be working on this for some time to come.

Why is it important? Not only is it the right thing to have our art and the people who make it accurately reflect society, but empowering different opinions in the room makes shows respectful, makes you realize blind spots you could never recognize for yourself and makes shows *better*.

I have seen specific situations where not having voices in the room led to horrible decisions. Most starkly, a Jewish comedy made without Jewish representation used a publicity image that unintentionally evoked the Holocaust. Unbelievable. And yet I didn't pick that up from the image either. Only by having appropriate representation in the room can these things be avoided.

Right at the start of my career I was drawing up lists of star actors for a role. It took a friend of mine from the global majority to question whether there was a reason they were all white. There wasn't at all, just an unconscious bias I wasn't aware of at the time. Hugely embarrassing. But something I was able to learn from.

Addressing this is not easy. You will lean on your immediate network when making a show. That probably means people from a similar background to yours. It requires significant conscious effort to build broad enough networks to address the problem. But those of us in positions of power must put in the work to do so.

Creative team

As in any business, charity, book club or sports team, people are the key to the success of your endeavour. The best people to employ might not be the most experienced or the highest profile. What you need is a little knowledge and a lot of enthusiasm. Making theatre can be stressful, and you need a team who help dissipate the stress, not contribute to it. They need to understand the scale at which they are working, and that everyone will be compromising.

Knowing who the best people are may seem impossible at this stage. But if you get your key appointments right then every person you employ will add their contacts and references to make it easier.

Director

The director is the most important member of your creative team. It will be your first appointment and along with them, you will find the rest of the team, cast the show and work together to make it happen. You will spend a lot of time talking to them, so don't engage someone who you don't get on with, however experienced they might be. That said, your director is the person who can elevate a project based on their experience and connections. So don't be afraid to reach for someone good. If they love the idea, who's to say whether they'll do it.

It's hard to judge directors. A director's job is to tell the story as clearly as possible. Some directors do that through flashy tricks, but others just take a script and work with the actors. Both types of directors can make good work. Don't presume someone isn't a good director because you can't see what they've added to a show. Most of their best work is invisible.

As such, you should look for someone who has a clear understanding of the script, and who you feel you can have a constructive working relationship with.

Other conversations to have with the director before you employ them include:

- How long do they need for rehearsals? Three weeks should be plenty for a play. Much more and it gets expensive. If your director is happy with two weeks for whatever reason, then great.

- Who are the designers they'd theoretically like to work with? It's unlikely that this will throw up obstacles, but it's worth knowing about. The director needs to be aware that if the designers won't work within the budgetary constraints, then you will need to find other people.

It is standard for the director to be employed until press night and then to be free to go and take other work. For a first-time producer it can be a bit of a shock to find yourself without your key collaborator after opening night. They may return once a week or so to give notes if they're particularly proud of it, but they are not obliged to. It's why it's important to build up a relationship with the cast and stage management, so they're comfortable with you after press night.

The same person directed both my first and second shows. Both shows were his idea. I had my concerns about them both creatively, but believed in him. The first, he stayed around the whole time, and brought over 100 members of the industry to see it (I know because I gave them all comps . . .). The second, he left after press night, and brought only three industry members. One was a hit, the other wasn't. I don't blame him for getting on with other projects after the second press night, but I wasn't expecting it at the time. I was left with the two actors and the stage manager on a show I knew wasn't good enough, and with a lot of seats to sell.

That was when I learnt that I had to believe in the show more than any other person.

Designer

This appointment should be led by the director. Most often the same designer will do both the set and the costume. This suits both parties as you only have to pay one person, and they get to have more control. Why costume and set are linked any more than lighting and sound is not particularly clear to me (possibly because the set design is done far in advance, so allowing time for costume?), but this is a common structure.

If the director has someone in mind, they should approach them in principle, before referring them to you to discuss money. You must be clear about the set and costume budget. It's vital they know the situation before they commit to the show. This may well be more important to them than their fee. They want to deliver something that looks great and will help their career.

If appointing a single designer, they're going to need some help. Probably a costume supervisor to help with costume sourcing. Discuss at the outset the workload/budget considerations. If they're involved to begin with, they'll help you solve the problem.

Lighting and sound designers

I put these in the same category because the process is similar. Both will want to see the kit list in the venue, and both will want to know their budget.

While it is possible to light a show using twelve lights, it doesn't give them much opportunity to 'design' anything. If you don't have money for hire (you probably won't), many designers are adept at finding lights for free, but need you to cover transport, and to take out sufficient insurance to cover them.

Lighting design is tricky as you don't get to see it until it is too late to change much. It's all the more important to appoint the right person. Your director and designer will lead this, but again, make sure you've talked budget with them before they're confirmed.

Sound designers tend to be the easiest to work with. Usually (but not always), the speakers in the venue are sufficient and they can design to them. But as per Chapter 3 on budgeting, make sure you've discussed kit, software and laptops before you begin.

Don't forget that all the designs should serve the show, rather than the show being about the designs. A good designer will do something beautiful to budget. A bad one will just keep asking for more money.

Casting director

Technically, this should be under my optional section later, but an experienced casting director is hugely valuable. We'll go through the casting in more detail shortly, but you're employing a good casting director for their contacts, organization and wisdom in auditions. A director may be able to do this, but often they just don't have the required knowledge base of actors.

Production team

The production team help implement and maintain the work of the creatives. They help make your life easier. They are worth getting on board as early as possible.

Production manager

The production manager is in charge of the physical production, including the production budget, set build and get-in. They will do all the necessary risk assessments and be in charge of health and safety, and organize production meetings.

The production manager is the most important appointment after the director. A good one will manage the designer and their expectations from an early stage and will save you money in the long run. Good ones are *hard* to find. So start early. The minute I've found a good one, they've been snapped up by the National Theatre or Punchdrunk.

It's possible to do it yourself, but know that their main body of work happens exactly when you should be selling the show hardest, and when rehearsals are at their most intense. The most consistent mistake I hear about from first-time producers is not appointing a production manager.

Stage management

In the West End this is a job for a number of people: company manager, stage manager, deputy stage manager and assistant stage managers. It's important to realize what a huge job it is, as for you it could be only one person. I'm a big fan of stage managers.

Company manager (CM)

The CM is in charge of the company and is the direct link to the producer. Their roles include making sure everyone arrives on time, being the point of contact for the theatre staff, managing absences (where there are understudies – unlikely for you) and managing morale.

Stage manager (SM)

The SM is in charge of the stage and anything happening on it. They are responsible for health and safety, rehearsal schedules, tech rehearsals, dress rehearsals and making sure the show happens each night.

Deputy stage manager (DSM)

The DSM cues the show from the 'book'. This means they have been in rehearsals noting every movement on stage, and sit through tech, noting every lighting or sound cue. They are then in charge of making sure these cues are executed on time at every performance.

Assistant stage manager (ASM)

ASMs are responsible for assisting the stage manager. Through rehearsals this is often buying the props for the show. Then during performances, they manage props, hold doors open and do anything and everything else backstage.

On a small show the stage manager often ends up taking on responsibility for all of this. It can be a huge amount of work. You as the producer/general manager can take on some of the company management duties, and the actors can often be persuaded to do without an ASM backstage. However, the duties of SM and DSM are always required. The role is usually referred to as 'company stage manager on book'.

And they're going to have to do the laundry. Or you are. This is one of those things that stage management shouldn't have to do. But you probably can't afford a wardrobe person, so you're going to have to find a way. Clear communication in advance and you'll be fine. Worth putting in their contract, so they know you're expecting them to handle it.

You need to watch your stage manager's hours. It can be an awful lot. When using union agreements, there are strong restrictions on how long they can work. You're unlikely to be using a union agreement, but that shouldn't impact the importance of ensuring they don't work themselves into the ground. Support them however you can, in particular through tech, dress and previews.

Like with a production manager, the day a stage manager comes on board means a drop-off in problems for a producer. Be nice to them, they will be there first, last, and receive the least credit. They are wonderful people. Treat them precisely the same as you do the actors and you'll be ok.

A horror moment in my career was watching an artistic director of a theatre deliver opening night cards to the actors and forgetting the stage management. Awful.

Other appointments

There are a number of other people that the director might ask for. Whether you need or can afford them is down to your budget.

- Assistant director – someone to help out the director. Totally optional. Not where I'd spend my money. Be very careful about work experience directors, they can't have *any* duties. They're just there to watch.
- Voice coach – they charge a lot per session, but you're likely to need only a couple of sessions if you need to support actors with specific accents. Make sure you know what it'll cost before you agree to it.

- Movement director/choreographer – will it make a noticeable difference to the show? More than that piece of set the director wants? Talk about it with the director in those terms and you'll find out how important it is pretty quickly.

- Composer – see above!

- Costume supervisor – these people are really useful. They source the costume on behalf of the designer. If your designer is doing both set and costume, when you get towards tech, a supervisor makes things much easier. But, of course, they need paying.

- Props supervisor – similar to costume supervisor, these guys source props on behalf of the designer. Unusual at the smaller scale, but may be cheaper than paying for an extra ASM for the whole run if the support is really needed.

- Production electrician/lighting programmer – often even if you're not employing these roles as members of the production team, your lighting designer will want them as part of their budget. This is all about clear communication at the outset with the lighting designer. They hang and focus the lights, and programme the lighting board. Same goes for production sound/sound programmer.

- Wardrobe supervisor – the person that manages the costumes on a daily basis. Unless you have a large cast with lots of costumes, someone you probably can do without.

Enthusiasm versus experience

In my experience it's almost always worth going for enthusiasm and commitment over experience, in all roles. If the experienced person is genuinely enthusiastic, that's fantastic, but avoid people doing it as a favour. However well intentioned, the person for whom the project is a big deal will always give it more attention, because they stand to gain more from it.

Summary

This is a fun bit of producing. Getting people who are excited about the show is so important. Never underestimate how excited they will get about it either. Whatever job it is we choose to do in this industry, we do it because we love theatre.

I still find myself surprised about how passionate the whole team can become. It sounds ridiculous when you write it down, but it's amazing how easy it is to forget. Even the person behind the box office at the theatre wants to work on a hit show. The biggest thing you can do as a producer is to create an environment where everyone is appreciated and where everyone can love your show like you do.

- Your director is the key to the process. Don't be afraid of reaching for someone big. If the script is good enough, why wouldn't they do it? They will then pull the project up to their level with everyone else they work with.

- Be led by your director on designers. But do your due diligence. Particularly if the director hasn't worked with them before. A difficult designer can ruin a project, even if two years ago they made something beautiful.

- Get a production manager. As soon as you can.

- Love your stage management. They're amazing people. (Can you tell yet that I used to be one?!)

- Say thank you. All the time. People run through walls making a show. Bigger and thicker ones if they feel like there's gratitude for doing it.

INTERVIEW WITH DIRECTOR JUSTIN AUDIBERT, ARTISTIC DIRECTOR OF CHICHESTER FESTIVAL THEATRE

Justin and I have been collaborators once, and good friends ever since. He has gone on to direct regularly at the Royal Shakespeare Company, run the Unicorn Theatre in London and is currently the artistic director of Chichester Festival Theatre. He spent a lot of his early career working in small venues.

Tim Johanson   Why did you work on the small scale?

Justin Audibert   Because those are the people who are going to give you a chance. One of the funny things about being a director is that most of the time, the first work you'll get offered is new. Most of the shows I did to start with came from writers who had seen something I'd done and then said, 'Would you be interested in doing my play?'

And then most of that work, because it's commercially risky, is going to happen in smaller venues, where you've got more of a chance of protecting those new pieces, whereas if you put it on a big stage, you're likely to expose it.

For a director, it's invaluable to have a smaller space because you can control the environment so much more. So actually to learn how lights work or how sound design impacts something. In a small environment it's easier to understand and then extrapolate into a bigger environment. It served me well anyway.

TJ   You can tell a story around a kitchen table.

JA   Exactly.

TJ   Any major drawbacks to working at that scale?

JA   I think there comes a point when you go, 'What could I do with more resource and on a bigger canvas and with more people watching it'. A hundred per cent.

And I know how important it is for you as a producer to have always paid people. But if you don't pay people properly they can't work at the level that you want them to. 'Cause they're juggling all these other things . . . and that's just talking about the quality of the work, aside from the morality of it.

TJ   With that mind, were there patterns to shows that went well or otherwise?

JA   There are three things I can think of. One is, as the director, could I carve out the time and the head space to really think the thing through? And sometimes on a smaller scale, you're going from job to job to job, you don't always get to do that.

Second, if the production manager, who often is in exactly the same position of doing too many things at the same time, is not available as much, that's a huge problem. The whole thing falls apart.

The third is, when you're the director, it's quite lonely and you are obviously with the cast and that's lovely, but you can't be too close friends because you have to be respectful and professional and all that stuff.

I always liked a producer who would challenge me, because when you're the director, you lose perspective on stuff sometimes. But knowing that they challenge you from a perspective of having your back at the same time. Whenever you felt like they don't have your back, they don't really care, if that, or any of those three things happen or go wrong, that's a problem.

TJ   What made you take on a show?

JA   This falls into two camps. After doing *Gruesome Playground Injuries* at the Gate Theatre, I made a decision to do shows that had a thing in them that I didn't know how to solve or I'd never done before. That was a distinctive decision and some of the times it was a real triumph and sometimes it was not a triumph!

After I'd made a series of those shows, then I had to make a choice about 'what do I really want to make?' What do I want to say that's a statement on the world and what I think of the world and why I make art.

TJ   So you were looking at the bigger picture rather than 'did it make me laugh' or the script itself?

JA   Yeah. Can I say something about the world with this thing? I'm a mission-orientated person. That was important to me.

TJ   How often were you originating stuff? Or were you always approached?

JA   A bit of both. Sometimes I would have an idea, sometimes it would be a producer, sometimes a writer. Mixed really.

TJ   What's the most important thing to get right in the casting process? Aside from taking direction, compatibility etc.?

JA   The number one thing is to make sure that whatever you are doing in the show is in the audition. So if they're going to be moving and dancing and singing and juggling on their head and unicycling make sure you've checked that in the audition. Anything like that, you should be clear that that's going to happen in the audition. And that they're game for that as well.

TJ   And what can a producer do to support the audition process or the casting processes?

JA   They are boring nuts and bolt things, the instruction of getting there in the first place. It being incredibly clear.

In an ideal world where possible you try and avoid people seeing others come in and out. Everybody wants you to do your best audition even if you're not right for that part, so set them up for the best audition. If you're in a line with ten other people, you're already going in with quite a negative mindset.

Asking people in advance to declare if they have any additional needs, access requirements.

It's useful to have an actor read the other parts. Unless you are really confident sight reader as a casting director or producer, just pay an actor fifty quid to come in and do it for a few hours.

And think about how you set the room so that it's not intimidating, for example, it's not a long walk down to meet you. Just make it as human as possible so that people can do their best work.

TJ How can a producer support a successful rehearsal period?

JA Like I said, it feels lonely sometimes. So constructive support and challenge is the key to everything. The more the producer is in the room, the better it is.

TJ Really?

JA Yeah, it's way better because everybody goes 'that person's really invested in the thing'. I'm not saying what you want is the producer to be chipping in when you're directing mid-scene. A hundred percent don't do that. But everybody seeing that that person is invested in the show is huge.

Just presence, that sitting in the room, being there at the end of the week, popping in. It's so important.

TJ How important is the actual room, if you're having to make rehearsal room versus set budget-type decisions?

JA That's tricky because rehearsal rooms are crazy expensive a lot of the time, but I also know what it's like to be in a damp or a cold room – it's horrible. There's a bit of a balance there. I think you can always do nice things that's like make sure there's tea, coffee and the kettle works and stuff and that.

TJ What's the key? Like enough room . . .

JA Enough room, some natural light, warmth, tea, coffee, good toilets and then not too crazy far away from a tube, train station, or whatever else. Thinking about people walking home at night in winter is also hugely important.

TJ Same question about tech through previews. How can a producer best support?

JA Until you get to dress rehearsal you kind of just need to get out the way. And then you should be judicious as a producer because dress rehearsal and first preview are two different things.

Make your notes in the dress rehearsal. But hold your fire into the first preview because basically it's Mike Tyson. Everyone's got plans, until they're punched in the face, and the audience will always punch you in the face.

And then that's the big time for a producer's input and support, from first preview to opening. Check you're aligning on the big things and challenge on those things.

TJ   What do you see the producer's relationship is with the creative of the show generally?

JA   The producer has to give the notes to the director and the director has to then give them to the company. That's important.

But I welcome notes. Notes are really good. Notes are how you get better. Doesn't matter who you are. So should a producer give notes to a director? A hundred percent. You might not always take them, sometimes you'll disagree. But it's weird to me when that doesn't happen.

TJ   What's your relationship as director to a show once press night is done?

JA   I mean it's odd. There's definitely a bit where you need to let the actors have the show and own the show, and there's definitely a bit where you can't let it go too. It's complicated. Probably the director should come back once a week is the way it should work.

TJ   When you've had a good relationship with producers, what's gone well?

JA   When it's gone well is where you've a hundred percent believed they've had your back and that all they care about is the show being good, and it's not about ego or any of the other stuff. I think it's almost as simple as that.

And that care has been shown for the company so that you're not dealing with the dressing room being damp . . . that stuff stopping the work from being good is a real problem as a director.

When it's clear how much it means to them, how much they just want show to be good – it's great.

8

Casting

There's conventional wisdom that 70 per cent of good directing is casting. Some people may say even more than that. I don't know if it's entirely true, but on the one occasion I've worked with a director who, it transpired, didn't understand the script, we were able to fix the show because we'd got the casting right.

Finding the right people is one of the most exciting parts of putting on a show. You might know who is going to be in your cast before you begin. Which is fantastic. But if you don't – let's dig in.

Casting is a three-step process:

- Who is theoretically right?
- Who is practically available and interested?
- Who is best for the role?

Auditions will answer the third question, but there's some work to do before that.

Who is theoretically right for a role?

The starting place is to draw up a list of actors who might theoretically be good in the role. This is known as a casting list. Your casting director will lead on creating it if you have one. If not, you and the director can do it.

Start with people you know of. That you've worked with, or seen perform on stage or TV.

Then, unless you've already found the perfect option, you can send out a 'casting breakdown'. This is a description of the project, the roles you are looking for and the fee. Anyone submitted by an agent in response to a breakdown is generally realistic, so you're not wasting time on people who are never going to do it.

In the UK it's done through a casting software called Spotlight. Hopefully, your venue, director or casting director has a subscription, if not you can sign up for a couple of months. You can send this breakdown to everyone on the database, to all talent agencies or to just a selection of agencies.

While sending out open breakdowns to everyone is commendable, I've done it only once and had over 600 submissions for a forty-plus-year-old-male role. Who knows how many it would have been for a younger role? That quantity is overwhelming, so more often than not people filter by agency – agencies have a lot of talented people on their books. This is why the only open casting calls you see are for big shows. They require big resources to sift through everyone.

Who is practically available and interested?

Once you have your lists, you select the top fifteen or twenty for each role and check whether they are available. This is an 'availability check', or 'AV check'. It involves contacting their agent and asking for their client's availability. You can presume that people submitted to a breakdown are available.

You might get told someone is technically available, or technically unavailable – this is an agent suggesting it's complicated!

An actor being available is *not* the same as the actor being interested! Agents for A-list stars will probably tell you their availability . . .

For those actors on your list that haven't been submitted, you'll need to establish if they're likely to be interested. Conversations with the agent will get you only so far; your casting director might have an idea – it's not an exact science. Ultimately, you'll find out through the next stage.

Who is best for the role?

Once you've established your list, you have two options.

Offer the role to your top choice directly. Or more likely, hold auditions.

Auditions

There are countless examples of auditions in popular media. The director and producer sit behind a desk, an actor comes in delivers their speech to an uninterested director, is cut off before the end and is sent on their way.

This isn't reality (or definitely shouldn't be!). Auditions are essential, but can be horrible experiences for performers. It is vital to make the experience as positive and inviting as possible. If you have one, your casting director will manage the audition process. If not, it's on you and the director.

The script needs to be sent in advance (two to three days ideally) with instructions as to whether to perform a specific section, or to read and choose a section of their own. It's not acceptable to send scripts/briefs the night before, actors shouldn't have to prepare into the early hours. Actors should each be allotted a ten-to-twenty-minute slot. Build in breaks through the day, casting is intense and you're likely to run behind.

Unless it's a monologue, someone will need to read the other parts. This shouldn't be you or the director. It's hard to watch the audition if you're reading with the actor. Consider asking someone to come and read for the day, or have the casting director help. Acting is about bouncing energy off another person, so whoever it is, make sure they show some enthusiasm!

Once you've seen everyone you can then offer the role or hold recalls. Recalls vary in style, but their purpose is to check the chemistry between actors or allow the director to work with people at greater length. Be led by your director and casting director.

Once you know who you want, ring the agent (or actor directly, if unrepresented) and offer them the role. You will need to confirm the fee, full dates of performances and rehearsal dates. You must give them a deadline by which to accept. Many agents stall acceptances on smaller shows in case something more lucrative comes in.

If you have an offer out to someone, you need to make sure you have a no before you move on, or at least let the agent know that because you haven't heard anything you're moving on. It would be a horrible situation to have two people think they have the role.

And as they all say yes, you are cast!

Letting actors go

Historically, the entertainment industry has auditioned actors, appointed the favourite and moved on with the project without bothering to inform all the auditionees. It was understood that a yes would happen fast and after a little while you'd just presume you hadn't got it. These days this is pretty universally regarded as unacceptable behaviour.

Every actor who came in will be waiting for the call saying they've got the role. As soon as you know they haven't, do them the courtesy of letting them know. It's ok to explain you're still considering them if you need more time, but once you've made your decision, let people know.

If actors ask for feedback, it's nice to give something. Actors rarely give bad auditions. They're usually just not quite what you're looking for. It's ok to say that. You'll soon work out that there are lots of actors who could play every role.

Representation

I've talked about representation in the chapter on creative teams. Exactly the same principles apply in casting. If your creative team is diverse, you will have fewer biases (conscious or unconscious) to overcome in casting.

Some roles in a show might be specific in a particular characteristic required – perhaps the character uses a wheelchair, or has a particular ethnic heritage. In which case you can place clear boundaries on casting.

Where the roles are not bound in such a way is where your biases are likely to be most exposed. One way to address this is to quota your auditionees. If you see a balanced spectrum of people at auditions, you are more likely to end up with a balanced cast. The cis, straight, white, able-bodied actor will still be seen, but the proportion seen will reflect society rather than the historic over-representation.

Hopefully, it goes without saying, but make sure any audition room is accessible for all those you would like to audition.

Musical casting

Musical theatre casting follows the same basic pattern as play casting, but the auditionee is likely to sing, and where required, may need to learn a dance.

You will need to have a room with a piano in it and someone skilled to play. The auditionee will arrive with a song of their choosing and the audition pianist will sight-read it. It may be that your team want to teach a bit of a song from your show; this should be stated in advance as people take different lengths of time to learn. Someone's ability to pick up a song in an audition context is no indication of their ability to be great in the role.

I did a workshop with an experienced, brilliant, actor who said that they would learn their lines before they arrived and wouldn't be able to pick up new stuff in the room as a result of their severe dyslexia. They were the most talented person in the room, but if they hadn't the experience and confidence to reach out in advance, we may have put them in a position where they couldn't have shown that. It would have been a failing of the process, not them.

Star casting

At some point in putting together a show, someone will say, 'Why don't we cast someone famous?' And they'll have a point. It will help with everything – with press, marketing, sales, the show's profile, the director's profile, your profile . . . it's remarkable the difference it makes – just take a look at the West End or Broadway.

The question is, how much of an artistic payoff there is for casting someone based on their profile? And if the answer is none, that they're also the best at what they do, how can you actually achieve it?

In the Venn diagram of 'famous' and 'good' relating to actors, there is absolutely a sweet spot in the middle of people who are well known and also good. Judi Dench, Benedict Cumberbatch, Sheridan Smith, Chiwetel Ejiofor and many others are fantastic actors, who as a result have become famous. They are also the most popular to employ.

Presuming you aren't going to get them at your scale, you're left in a situation looking for one of three things:

- Blind luck that you are friends with said person and they (and their agent) are up for the job
- Compromising on the artistic quality
- A clever casting of someone who'll be brilliant, who is well known, but isn't an established theatre name

I've seen all three of those options (the second *all* the time). The third is the most likely, and so long as the director is onside, you have the time and a backup plan, it is worth pursuing.

On an early show in my career a casting director managed to persuade Ardal O'Hanlon to do an Off-West End show. He was a well-established name due to his TV profile, but had few stage credits. What we were offering was something that presented him as a serious theatre actor. He was brilliant in the role, and absolutely made the difference in terms of sales. His getting involved in that show launched my career. For his part, the casting director for the Donmar Warehouse came to see the show, and his subsequent role there won him an Olivier Award nomination. So there was benefit to both sides.

How do you go about it? Draw up a list with your director and/or casting director and work out *realistically* who is perfect. Your casting director will help with the realistic bit.

Think about how you could make a case for your number one target. Then, ideally, find a route to contact them directly. If you can't find one, ring their agent, and clearly make your case. You never know. Bear in mind, you are not asking them to read or audition, you are making an offer. Your director will want to meet them for a mutual 'chemistry' session, but that takes the form of a coffee, not a reading.

Don't discount the fact that you don't have a big theatre. So don't think that you need to have the same calibre of person that is required to sell a 1,000-seat house. If you can persuade someone who does tons of quality theatre, even if they're known only within the industry, it might transform your production. The critics will take note and regular theatregoers will notice it. And if they do tons of theatre, they'll be really good.

If the agent doesn't dismiss the enquiry out of hand, they will ask for you to send through the details and the script, which they will then forward onto their client. This process can take a while. If you're approaching someone successful, they will be busy, and the agent will not want to bother them. Put a timescale on it. Ask if their client will be able to look at it within a week. This is an easy way of wasting time on unrealistic prospects. That's why you need to be sure they are realistic.

Unfortunately, you likely won't be able to start this process until six months out. The agent won't even consider it – they're expecting far more lucrative offers. If you can get to the actor directly, all of these problems are much easier. Negotiating agents is a real skill.

If you do get interest from an actor with a high profile that's great. They will be doing it because they love the show, no other reason. So when the agent starts asking for private cars, press fees, private dressing rooms or whatever else, know that their client is doing it for the show, not for any of the other reasons. Whether you can accommodate those requests is up to you, but you *can* say no. They're not doing a small show for the money or perks.

Summary

I love casting. It's creative, it's fun and performers consistently show such talent.

- Use a casting director if you can. Even if it's just for their lists of people – it's a huge help.
- Ensure your director makes for a warm, inviting and inclusive audition room. People find auditions stressful, it's vital you don't contribute to that.
- Do actors the courtesy of letting them know they haven't got it.
- Acknowledge your unconscious biases in who you're looking at. A more diverse industry will be a stronger industry.
- Try to find a way to make star casting a bonus, not essential. If it is essential, don't sign the venue deal until you have it.

INTERVIEW WITH TALENT AGENT ALEX SEGAL, MANAGING DIRECTOR OF INTERTALENT

Alex is the managing director of the leading talent agency Intertalent. Having worked his way up from the bottom, he is the youngest managing director in the company's thirty-year history, and a supremely experienced agent.

Tim Johanson   How does the relationship work between an actor and an agent?

Alex Segal   It's a team. My responsibility is to create opportunities and to protect my client. Nowadays, there's a huge amount more that goes into the agent/client relationship but ultimately it all comes back to that.

You both need to be on the same page with a strategy. For my clients, it's a one-year, three-year, five-year plan. You can never predict what's going to happen in this industry. But what you can think about is, is this job going to get me to where I want in one year, three years, five years?

As an agent, can you create possibilities for them? Can you guide them? And are you on the same page as to where you want to get to? And if all of those are a tick, and you have the right relationships, you're going to have a great long-term partnership.

TJ   How does the one-year, three-year, five-year plan work?

AS   It's about agreeing on short- and long-term goals from the outset. Coming back to the basics of it, just like in producing, there's no rules. But my belief, the way I've been taught and the way that I work, is that there are three reasons to do a job.

Number one is to actually enjoy it. People forget that, but it's important to actually have a good time. We're in one of the best industries in the world, enjoy what you do.

Number two, will you get paid? And will you get paid well? That helps, right? That's a key part of my job.

Number three, and maybe the most important, will this job get us the next job?

I'm happy to at least tick two of those boxes. If I'm ticking only one, or none, I'm asking 'why are we doing this?' We always need to agree on why we're saying yes to a project.

I can't dictate what auditions are going to come and when. I can't dictate who's going to say yes to giving you a job. All I can do is use my knowledge and network to create possibilities and then does the job that tick those boxes? If it does, then it's part of our plan. And it will get us to the promised land at some point.

TJ   How does theatre fit into that?

AS   When you're working with actors, theatre is an important part.
Nine times out of ten the money can't compare with TV & film.
Theatre is important, though, because theatre is where everyone
started. Even if that's at university or drama school, you start in
theatre, and therefore everyone has a special place for performing
in front of a live audience. Theatre is important to scratch that itch.
Playing to an audience is more exciting than playing to the camera
without a doubt.

TJ   And so, of your three things, leaving money out, you'd want
for your clients for it to be a great job, have fun, scratch the itch.
And then people come and see them so it can help them with the
next one.

AS   Yes. There's a feeling that you do your greatest work on stage. And
I would definitely agree with that.

TJ   There is an old quote I can't quite remember about film is for fame,
TV's for money and stage is for soul.

AS   One hundred per cent.
   Listen, if you're a very famous person, then theatre can be all
of the above. But you know, if you're at the National Theatre on a
favoured nations wage, that's ok. Most people would work there for
free. That is the pinnacle as an actor.

TJ   Bearing in mind that most people reading will consider the
National Theatre and the wages they pay as the upper limit of what
was in scope, how do you see small-scale theatre? Fringe festivals,
Off-West End and so on. How and when do they fit?

AS   I'm generalizing. But there's two kinds of situations. You're either
at the start and you're building your experience and relationships, or
you're more established.
   For young actors who are developing it's great because it gives
you a place to broadcast your talent and take risks. For actors who
don't need to work at the smaller scale, it is still important because it
gives people the chance to be creative, to experiment, to be as artistic
as they can be. Because actually when you get more established, the
chances to just have fun don't come every day. And even if you earn
good money on TV or play the National, going into a small-scale
venue for a couple of months on basically no money is still where I
find my actors have had a hell of a time.

TJ   Does it change any of those answers if someone has profile?

AS   The rule often is: the bigger you become as an actor, the less you
work.

TJ   Really?

AS   Yeah. When you become big, you can't say yes to anything and
everything, you can't always do the things that gives you the soul.
Because when you get to a certain level, you're expected to be at that

level. And being at that level doesn't always, as far as the industry's concerned, mean it's right for your image to play smaller theatres. And that's not just about theatre, that's TV and film as well.

The bigger you become, the fewer jobs you take. And also, the fewer the jobs come, because people think you won't do it. Or people think you're too big for them, or too busy. People just assume that they don't want to work. They're too busy. They're too rich. Actually, actors do want to work. But they're scared at times about their 'brand' or if it gets bad reviews. So, you have this weird thing where you could be a top actor, and literally do one job a year. And that's a combination of their own internal dilemmas, and part other people thinking they can't get them.

TJ   That's interesting. So you've got an actor, aside from the real big stars, because even getting them to the West End is a huge achievement, what you're saying is that you should make the offer, you should make the approach?

AS   Yeah. For sure.

TJ   Because they might not be being asked?

AS   Being an actor in theatre is the best way to prove your talent. I don't necessarily agree with that, but put it this way – an actor gets more credit on a stage than they do in a soap.

TJ   How much does it make a difference whether you've heard of the person who's approached you?

AS   This industry is about relationships. As a budding producer, the more people you know, the more people you meet, the easier it is. For young producers, network hard. Go to every show, go to every event, industry, master class, wherever.

I protect my client. The last thing you want is a producer who says they've got money but doesn't. As an agent, my number one thing is just transparency with the producer. If the show isn't fully funded, just say that. If the client loves it enough, they'll still attach to it.

Actually, attaching (someone to a show) is a great way to sort of scratch each other's backs. If you're attached to a play, what you're saying is, my actor will put their name to this.

So when you go to fundraise, or go to a venue, you can say that this person has strong interest. And if it comes off, you have to come to us first. We might not agree a deal, but you have to come to us first. So you scratch my back; I'll scratch yours.

TJ   And so, let's say I'm a new producer, it's essential that I get someone who can sell some tickets. What's the best way of me legitimizing myself to you? Is it about trying to buy you coffee? Is it about trying to get a coffee with your client with no commitment? Is it about sending you an email with the references and last people I worked with?

AS So here are the stages. If it's a producer that I've not worked with before and doesn't come with big reputation, first things first, I would look at how they've approached. How do they write? Receiving 300 emails a day, you quickly get a sense of what's serious and what isn't.

Then I'd have a chat with them on the phone. I say, tell me more. Is it funded? What's your plan? What's your budget? Where are you going? Everything. If I feel like it's real, and I have to be honest, nine out of ten things that I deal with never see the light of day. If I feel like this could be of interest to my client, I'll always take it to them. Even if I'm not sure they should do it.

If the client is interested. Then we'll do a meeting either with the client or without, depending on how confident I am about this person.

TJ So, with that in mind, one of the big frustrations I have when I talk to agents is the insistence on dates. It's the chicken and egg of producing. You can't get the theatre until you've got the star. But you can't get the star without dates from the theatre.

AS Dates. Dates are key. There's no point working on things when the actor's not free.

Agents will always ask for dates because there's so many things going on that might or might not happen. Things are always just hanging in the balance and dates are a step towards something actually happening. It's always a conversation. It's about openness.

But I think the chicken and egg thing is the biggest problem. Try and be as far along the process as you can be before needing to come to an agent.

TJ When you make an offer to a star, you typically need to allow three weeks for someone to read a script. What's going on in that three-week period?

AS Probably one of a couple of things. One, the actor might be busy, and can't read it straight away, two that agent might not get around to it straight away or three, they're not sure what to do and need to think about it. But yeah, if you're going to go out to star names, you have to be prepared to sit and wait. It's a game of cat and mouse.

TJ It's a problem, though, when you've got the dates . . .

AS It's a big problem. But be open. You might say I'm out to a few people in one go.

TJ Really?

AS Yeah. I might not be happy with you saying that, but you could say to me, 'Look, I'm going out to three-star names, but I need my person within three weeks'. You can put the pressure on me. I'll try and disarm the pressure, because I don't want pressure on me, I want to be putting the pressure on you . . . and I might call your bluff if I need more time. I have to be honest, I find it quite fun.

TJ Okay. I love that. I would never have done that before.

How do you feel about people approaching your clients directly?

AS Badly. If an actor has an agent and you're approaching that actor directly, at some point you'll get to the agent and you're going to have to start all over again. I feel like it's a waste of time doing that. Just because you've said 'the actor's told me they're interested', it doesn't mean it's going to happen. Because often people say things that you want to hear. And I get annoyed at my clients who do say that when they don't actually mean it. And now I'm the one that's going to have to get them out of this mess. So you're better off approaching the agent directly because it just becomes complex. And, the agent becomes slightly wary of you doing that.

TJ What happens if you know the client or the client is a friend of friends?

AS I would always say to my clients, 'Tell them to get in touch'. So I can start off by knowing that we're all trying to make this happen.

Agents aren't a necessary evil, they're necessary. We do an important job and good ones are not there to be difficult, we're there to make things go more smoothly.

TJ How much do you actually care about approvals? In trailers, photos etc.

AS I try and get as many approvals as I can because it allows us to get rid of things that we feel are detrimental. People are protective of how they look. We're in that world and the idea that we can approve a picture or whatever, I think that's fine.

There are a lot of things that need to be negotiated upfront. If my client won't talk to certain press, if my client isn't around to do press or if my client wants fifty tickets on opening night, we should talk about that early. Once you're contracted it's hard to go back. The power for us as an agent is in the negotiation. The last thing you want is to forget something or think about something after the fact. So, while we're negotiating, that's your one chance to get the right dressing room, to get the right travel, to get the right number of press night tickets, approvals. All of that.

What I would say to any emerging producer is try and come to an agent as late as possible, have as much in place as possible, be honest, communicative and transparent, and try and build that relationship. So coming to an actor should be in a weird way, one of the last things you do.

TJ This is the crux. With both smaller- and larger-scale theatre it's just not possible.

AS Yeah, because if you get the actor, you can then cement everything.

TJ This is the thing that I realized. What's the thing that green-lights a show? The actor. So I'm going to start there. This is why it's tempting to go direct because I don't think an agent is going to let that happen, unless you have a really good relationship. And I want to sit down with an actor and say 'what do you want to do?'

AS Yeah. I appreciate a producer will see this one way and an agent another, but if we have the same intentions we'll get a deal done.
   If you'll come to an agent at the beginning of the process, when nothing is set, you have to be even more honest and even more communicative than when it's ready to go.

TJ '. . .I think this client of yours should always have been on stage. They never have. Can we sit down and work out what that might look like?'

AS I don't mind attaching my clients to things early. But I want to know where you're going. I want to know which venues are going to suit because there might be some we don't want to work in. That's what I mean by being completely honest.
   Then maybe it's about being creative, can they be a producer on it? How can we get them to have the best time?

9

Contracts

From the highs of appointing your team and the excitement of casting to ... contracts.

Contracts are a vital annoyance. Get them done promptly after you've appointed each person, and move on with the show.

A contract is the agreed terms between two parties. A contract can be verbal, written on the back of an envelope, an email or, most often, a signed document. Two people saying to one another, 'Yes I agree to that', is a contract. Why we write it down is in case there's a disagreement.

The financial value of most theatre contracts means they are unlikely to end up in a court dispute; there simply isn't enough on the line. Theatre is made on goodwill; the contract is about clarity of intention and mutual understanding. Reputation and a sense of decency will determine whether contracts are honoured, not the threat of the law.

The value of having a contract is to avoid surprises. It's an exercise in expectation management. If you put two tickets on press night in the contract, then they shouldn't complain when you put that policy into practice. Likewise, if you put the length of rehearsals into the director's deal, you know they (probably) won't argue later.

Types of contracts

There are three types of contracts in theatre: a deal memo, a letter of agreement or a full-form contract. They are all valid, and, more or less, the same thing. An agent may ask for any of them.

A full-form contract is exactly that. Three to five sides of A4, which covers everything. They've possibly been looked at by a lawyer and are as detailed as possible.

A deal memo is an agreement that has the key points, the 'heads of terms', but not the details. The idea is that you come back to the full-form contract later. For your purposes the email exchange you've had with the person or agent negotiating will do – a deal memo is a glorified bullet-pointed email.

I'd suggest a simple letter of agreement. It's a letter written by you, which summarizes the agreement you've come to, and asks them to sign at the bottom. Some would consider it a deal memo, some a simple full-form contract! Ultimately, all of them serve the same purpose.

Remember you are signing this on behalf of the producing entity (your company), not yourself.

Essential details to include

- The show, the venue and the role. It's important to be clear, in particular if an actor or creative is taking on multiple roles.

- Dates. Provide a rehearsal, tech, preview and performance schedule. Creatives are contracted until press night, not thereafter. Cast and stage management are contracted until the end of the run.

- Money. What's the fee? And when is it going to be paid? Weekly is common for cast and stage management.

    The payment structure I often use for creatives is 33 per cent on signature, the same on first day of rehearsals and the final third on press night.

That's all you have to have in an agreement. There are more things that are useful to clarify, but once people know what the engagement is, what the dates are and how much they're being paid, they tend to be satisfied.

Other contract details

- Complimentary tickets. It's a good idea to get this in here. It manages expectations later. A pair for everyone on press night is my policy. More on this later.

- Having the right to make a video recording and take photos of the production. I've never had anyone being difficult about this. But if they were difficult, it'd be a disaster. You need the photos and video clips to promote the show, and an archive recording to send to relevant industry who missed it live. It's *not* ok for you to make money from any of this outside the production itself, without a further deal.

    If you do want to broadcast a video of the production and charge for it, you need a further agreement with everyone involved. If you already know you're going to do this, you can cover it in this initial agreement. A share of any income/profits is a fair way to do this as it insures you against there being limited income, and you're not asking anyone to do much, if any, extra work.

- A summary of the dressing room situation. The cast spend a lot of time in their dressing rooms, so make sure they know how good/limited they might be in advance.

The instinct with a contract is to try to put in everything possible. But things shift around, and the implicit understanding is that people will move with them. Don't try to cram too much into a deal. If an agent is insistent, then that's different. But in the initial offer, keep it simple. Just because you haven't said in the contract that they'll have their headshot on the venue website doesn't mean that they can't have their headshot on the venue website, but it means you don't *have* to (if the venue said 'that's not what we do', having this in the cast contracts would be a pain).

I'll come on to this more in the marketing section, but while it's ok to clarify *how* the creative will be billed, 'Director – Joanne Bloggs', and that they will be billed for all of their roles ('composer/sound designer' is a common one), it's not ok for them to specify *where* that will happen. For designers, stipulate that when the director is credited, they will be, and leave it at that. Again, if you can avoid putting this in there in any form, so much the better, it doesn't mean that you won't be fair later on.

Try not to agree to random approvals for the cast (or anyone). It's not something they actually expect, it's just something agents like to have, and it's a pain. If a star actor insists on photo approval, make sure that they *have* to approve a certain number – three at least. If not, an actor's vanity could derail your press and marketing campaign.

I produced a US playwright's play, and the agent insisted on cast approval, even though his client had no idea of any actors in the UK. When I sent our cast list to the playwright, he could not understand why we were asking him, he *obviously* wasn't the person to ask. It made us look incompetent. But the agent wanted it. So.

Negotiating contracts

Part of the job is negotiating these contracts. Nobody enjoys it. I particularly dislike doing it with creative agents.

Some agents have an implicit assumption that you're screwing their client, and are always looking for more. Others have a target figure they think is fair, and will push until they get that. And a few accept whatever you offer.

This is where the smaller and larger scales differ. When it's a small budget, you will be aware that people will have to accept less than their worth to work on your show. You will do everything you can to *increase* the budget line per creative, to show how much you value them.

Trying to establish which type of agent you're dealing with in advance is impossible. I've encountered all three. Offering the budget line to the first type results in your having to take money from elsewhere in the budget to satisfy them. The second group are much fairer and will understand your situation. And if you offer below the budget line to the third group, in the expectation that they're going to push you up, and they accept, you feel like you're screwing your creative.

I recommend going in 10 per cent to 15 per cent below your budget line and allowing yourself to be pushed up. It helps the agent look good for their client, and you get to keep your budget in check.

As we talked about when budgeting, it's a good idea to do the deals in the order – director, designer, lighting designer, sound designer. No designer's agent thinks it's ok for their client to be paid the same as the director. Therefore, the director's deal sets the ceiling. Likewise, the lighting designer is not going to be paid more than the designer, so the designer's deal is your ceiling there.

The best you can do is your best. The key to any negotiation is to be prepared to say no. If money is the sticking point, and you can't go any further, try to reduce the time someone is required. If you can't agree terms there will be another person out there. Be firm, and the agent will agree pretty quickly. Time is the main pressure here, so get on with the deal as soon as you can.

Cast deals are simpler, particularly if you have provided the fee to agents during the casting process and as long as you're paying everyone the same (which you should be). Similarly with stage management, they will want to know the fee before they come to interview, so by the time you're doing the contract there's little to discuss.

Agents work for their client, not the other way around. So, however difficult they are being, know that if your creative wants to do the project, you will find an agreement. If you can't? They were the wrong creative for your show.

Summary

I don't know of a single producer that sets out to screw their team through negotiations. I know of many who haven't done negotiations early enough, thereby leaving expectations unmanaged with the artist. That's where problems arise. Get the contract done as soon as you can.

- A contract is *any* agreement between two people.
- Their central purpose is to manage expectations.

- Don't overcomplicate the agreement.
- Remember the agent works for the client, not the other way around. Either they want to do the gig or not.

Not the most fun bit of producing this. But really important.

10

Management

Appointing your team is a huge step. You have just increased the skill set on the show many times over. Your job now is to make sure everyone is working in the same direction, and to make sure they're doing it within budget. You've employed them to be brilliant, now it's about supporting them so they can be. You're also going to start flexing your cheerleading muscles. As soon as people start work, they're going to need encouragement.

Trust the people you've employed. Be aware of what they're doing and be prepared to step in if required, but your baseline assumption should be trust. If it isn't, you've appointed the wrong people.

We're going to look at the design process and production meetings. Outside of casting and selling the show, these are the bedrock of the weeks before rehearsals begin. We're going to talk about accountancy, plus the programme, as it's a bigger job than you're expecting.

Managing the design process

After you've appointed your team, and before rehearsals start, the design process will get underway. Your director should lead this.

Usually set design needs to be done first, so it dominates early discussions. Costume and sound come to a peak during rehearsals, as that's when decisions are made, and realistically you won't see the lighting design until you're in the theatre.

Your production manager will help manage the set design process. The designer and the director will chat creatively, but your production manager should know what's going on. The production manager should be running a budget as to how the set will be built.

Good production managers will keep you updated – be wary if things go quiet. The situation you're watching out for is the designer and director getting carried away and your production manager being busy with other projects. You need to make sure what is being designed is feasible. A good designer should know this.

Once you get towards rehearsals, it becomes difficult to change the set design. The designer will build the model box (a cardboard scale version of the set), and the production manager will cost how much it will be to build. The bigger the set, the further out the design must be finalized. If you're cobbling together something that doesn't require a build, then it can come later. As I mentioned in the budgeting section, one of my favourite designs was a series of strip lights, some rubble and six chairs. It cost £200 and was assembled in an hour at the get-in.

Costume can start in earnest once a designer has measurements from the cast. This is often day one of rehearsals, but if you get everyone together for a publicity photo shoot in advance, that's a great time to get measurements.

Managing the costume process is budgetary management. They should have a budget per costume, and should be talking to you if there's a particularly expensive item they need. If you're renting costumes, you'll be involved in negotiating prices. For some reason production managers don't engage with costume in the way they do other design departments, meaning I've often worked more closely with the costume team than anyone else.

In an ideal world a sound designer will be in many rehearsals, building their design around the work in the room. This is an expensive use of time. The reality is usually somewhere between that, and just coming to watch a run of the show in the final week of rehearsals.

The lighting designer will come to see the first run that they're able to, and extrapolate their initial thoughts into a specific design from there. You'll see what they've been up to in tech.

You should be receiving regular spending updates from the production manager or from the designers directly. If you don't, be prepared for people to go over the budget without telling you, or even without noticing themselves. I've been presented with brown envelopes full of receipts before now, and heard horror stories of a props budget going three times over budget and nobody knowing until receipts were presented halfway through the run. This is where finding the balance between micro-management and trusting people is key. It's reasonable to have a weekly budgetary update from all departments.

Production meetings

Production meetings are regular meetings with the creative and production team to check on progress. They are key.

Attending should be the designers, the director, the production manager and you. Other attendees could include the stage management, costume supervisor, fight director or anyone who isn't the cast. They should be chaired by the production manager.

The agenda should include:

- The state of the designs
- The budget department by department
- The schedule for the get-in and technical period
- Pre-rehearsals, the rehearsal set-up and rehearsal progress once they've started.

Production meetings are great for shared help and expertise. They are essential at all levels of theatre to ensure things aren't being missed. You should hold your first one once you have the whole team, but no later than three weeks before the start of rehearsals, then one on the first day of rehearsals, and weekly thereafter. Pre-rehearsal meetings can be held online, which saves a lot of travel time.

Accounting, bookkeeping and payroll

You need to keep track of money. You will need to pay everyone, to prepare accounts at the end of the show and to have business accounts signed off for HMRC.

Larger productions use a bookkeeper, a production accountant and a chartered accountant to do each of these. The only one you need is someone legally able to do your business accounts at the end of the year. Everything else needs to be accurately monitored and presented for the purpose of open-book accounting, and for investors and funders, but you can do it.

Bookkeeping is keeping track of what's been spent. There aren't hundreds of transactions on a small production, and most of them are done by the production and design team. Keep an accurate spreadsheet of what's been spent, and from which budget, and you'll be fine. Then cross-check with the bank account to make sure the spreadsheet equates with reality.

Payroll is paying people. When contracts become complicated and cast and stage management larger in big productions, it's a time-intensive job that requires a specialist. For small shows, it is the case of paying invoices when they land. I have never used anyone else to do my payroll.

I panicked on my first show when an agent asked me for a remittance slip. I said 'of course' but didn't have a clue what one was. I rang a friend and he explained. It's a reverse invoice. In case you wondered. You send it to tell someone you've paid them, with all the same details as their invoice. Ten plus years on and I've never sent one since.

Programme

It often happens during rehearsals, but the programme is worth getting started early as it's a big job.

Having some sort of programme is essential. Your company are doing the run for the benefit of their careers, and it's vital that anyone coming to the show knows who they are. It can be an A5 piece of paper with their names. Or it can be a sixteen-page glossy programme. Everyone prefers the latter; you just have to make sure you get the costs right. It's a lovely keepsake for the show. Done right, it can also be an income stream.

Essential to include

- A credit for *everyone* involved in the production
- Biographies for any creative, including actors, designers etc. Get these from everyone at the time you employ them if you can.

I prefer a list of credits, but some productions turn these into a piece of creative writing. Either way, provide them with a word limit. Have a standardized format for these (italics, capital letters, which punctuation to use, etc.) Expect 25 per cent to ignore the word limit and 95 per cent to ignore the standardized format.

It's not the *first* change I'd make if I was Grand Lord Of All Theatre, but pretty soon after my appointment I'd standardize biography formatting for all in our industry. The endless hours I've spent re-formatting programme biographies . . .

Maybe this is an opportunity. If you're reading this and have a biography:

- Capitals and italics for titles of shows: *Cat On A Hot Tin Roof*
- Brackets for venue: *Cat On A Hot Tin Roof* (National Theatre)
- Commas between credits: *Cat On A Hot Tin Roof* (National Theatre), *The Tempest* (Southwark Playhouse)
- No roles. Sorry actors.
- Production companies only for screen and radio, not theatre.
- No CAPITALS, semi colons, different fonts, pdfs or anything funky that you think looks good. Leave that to the graphic designer please.

Much obliged.

Optional to include

- Cast headshots
- Rehearsal room photos (make sure you have each of the team featured in at least one picture)
- Biographies for the production team. It's typically not expected. But some people do.

Printing
- B5 is the West End size; A5 is cheaper, and should be fine.
- They will likely be eight, twelve or sixteen pages. Sixteen is often cheaper than twelve due to folding or printing or something. You need to come up with all the content and the design.

Plan to make money on the programme, or at least break even. Expect to sell one for every seven or eight tickets sold. Expect to give 30 per cent of your venue capacity's worth away to press on press night (up to a maximum of 50-ish?), plus one free for everyone in the team. Your venue is going to want a commission for selling them (see Chapter 3 on venue contracts). Don't order too many, you can always order a top-up if you're selling lots of them.

Directors sometimes write a piece in the programme on their interpretation of the play, known as a director's note. Around the time I was producing my first show, I read a bad review of a play where the reviewer spent a good amount of the review talking about how they did not want to be told what to think about a show in the programme. I took this as a sign not to have them. Put in some more rehearsal photos.

When you have a proof of the content, have each person on the team check their biography to make sure they're happy before you go to print.

Summary

There doesn't seem like a great deal here, and there isn't really. But you're also pulling together your team, employing a press rep, managing the marketing campaign and starting the sales strategy. And you're preparing for rehearsals. So just make sure it doesn't get forgotten.

All fun though.

- No news in the design process is almost always bad news. People love telling you when they've done something. Quiet usually means they haven't. Bear in mind you're unlikely to be paying them enough for their exclusive time, so stuff can get lost across multiple jobs.
- Accounting is an *every week* thing, not an *after the run is over* thing.
- Start the programme earlier than you're expecting, it takes ages and can be a painful process. Your team *care* about it. So get it right.

11

Rehearsals – the magic begins . . .

This is where it all starts to get real. You've employed a great team to bring your great script to life. Now they start to do their thing and you float to the edges. You've employed professionals to do their job, and they will. Your focus should be on selling the show. You also need to make sure the company are happy and rehearsals are going smoothly. If it isn't, you'll want to know asap.

Rehearsals are where your director is going to prove their worth. Your role as a producer is limited, and it's important that you give the director space. How much space? I've never watched a rehearsal in my career that I wasn't invited to. But would expect to be there at the beginning or end of the day to show support two to three times a week. You've got a marketing campaign to be running, remember.

Rehearsal room

Hiring a rehearsal room is easy if you have money. If you don't, it requires ingenuity. Have your director be part of the discussions, it's their room. If they'd rather save some money here and spend it elsewhere, that's their call.

The key factors:

- Not too hot or cold. If you're rehearsing in the height of summer or winter, be particularly conscious of this.
- Not too inconvenient to get to.
- Big enough to fit the whole stage in. On day one the stage manager will 'mark up' the stage with tape on the floor so that the rehearsals can be conducted in the correct space.
- For a musical it may be necessary to have a sprung floor and mirrors, you might need particular sound equipment or a piano. These all cost more.
- Access requirements appropriate for your company – most obviously wheelchair access, but ensure you have asked what requirements

might be and have catered for them. If you're booking a rehearsal room in advance of casting (often the case), limited access will start restricting who you can cast.

In an ideal world:

- Access to a green room/kitchen in order for people to make lunch.
- An extra space for costume fittings. It allows the cast and creatives to work in a comfortable environment. This is a luxury many shows don't have.
- Exclusive hire – you can leave your set and your markup for the whole rehearsal period. Non-exclusive hire is a burden on the team in terms of finishing promptly, and clearing everything away. Similarly:
- Same room throughout the process. Moving rooms adds stress, time and cost – but can be done if absolutely necessary.

When looking for a room, don't discount the bigger rehearsal groups. As they have more income (and are often charities), they can do deals for emerging companies. They've often been the best option for me, as people love rehearsing there and the cost has been equivalent to somewhere much worse.

If you end up in a less-than-perfect room, think of ways you can improve it: scheduling rehearsals so travel is at off-peak times, fruit, biscuits, coffee and tea, stationery – little bits to make the room more pleasant.

Rehearsal set, props and costume

Rehearsals will require props and possibly bits of set in order to rehearse properly. Your production manager will help with set or set replica; stage management will source props. Vital requirements for rehearsals should be flagged in a pre-rehearsal production meeting.

A common situation is that you're creating an innovative bit of set, but the director needs a replica in rehearsals. Your budget can only just about cope with the real one. The easiest way to do this? Recognize early enough, get it built early and get the real one into the rehearsal room for the final week of rehearsals. This won't cost much extra, it just requires planning. If it's that important, it'll also save you a bunch of time in tech as everyone will be used to it. Alternatively you'll need to adjust your tech schedule to accommodate extra time rehearsing with the set piece.

First day of rehearsals

The first day of rehearsals traditionally brings everyone together for a read-through of the script and a showing of the set model box. The standard schedule for the day is half an hour of meet and greet (it's a nice idea to provide coffee/tea and biscuits), then a model box showing with the set designer, followed by a full read-through of the script for everyone present. This can usually be done before lunch at which point all those not required for rehearsals can leave. A production meeting and costume measurements are often done this day too.

This day allows as many people as possible to have met one another, and to allow the whole team to hear the script in its barest form. It's useful as an exercise for the designers to focus on the script and any issues it throws up, it allows you to get the first feel as to what the production will eventually be like and, most importantly, it's the first time to enthuse everyone about what a fantastic show it's going to be.

Some directors don't like a read-through. That's their prerogative. You should still have a meet and greet and a model box showing.

This is also the time that the Safe Space guidelines should be outlined. This is an Equity initiative designed to ensure rehearsal spaces are a safe, secure working environment. Generally, this is led by stage management, but you should be active in making this a priority. Both UK Theatre and Equity have resources you can look up.

Rehearsal reports

Each day the stage manager will compile a report of everything that's come up in the room that day and circulate it to everyone on the show aside from the cast. You should read these every day, as they're the best indicator of what's going on in the room. The design team will be expecting these, so it's important you make sure the stage manager is doing them – 99.9 per cent will do so automatically.

Rehearsal schedule

This is the preserve of the director. Some directors want to work 9am to 7pm, some 10am to 5pm. Some want to work all day Saturday, while some are content with Monday to Friday. I've no idea if there would be a correlation between the response to a show and the intensity of its rehearsal. What I do know is that your actors must buy into it. Actors want to have done enough rehearsal to be comfortable on stage. One particular show I did, the two actors begged me and the director to do additional Saturday and evening rehearsals.

Generally the cast become comfortable quickly and don't appreciate overdoing rehearsal. Most directors are great about it and I've never had to step in. Where there have been problems, the company have raised something to the director and stage manager, who have solved it.

Rehearsal room runs

Towards the end of rehearsals, the director will run the play from start to finish. Some of these runs will be closed, just for the core rehearsal team, and some will be open to everyone.

Go to the first rehearsal room run that you're invited to. I missed a first run once and the company decided that I wasn't interested in the show. I went to the second (as I'd always planned), but never recovered their trust. It was a troubled show, but was a lesson in the importance of showing interest and enthusiasm.

Rehearsal social events

I like to arrange one or two social 'events' during the rehearsal period. Once the show is open, the director and design team will disappear and you will be left with just the cast and stage management. An organized (optional) trip to the pub, in the first and last weeks of the run, is a great opportunity to get to know everyone. Offering to buy the first round usually gives me a good turnout. It also serves as an opportunity for anyone to have a quiet word if something is up in the rehearsal room. If you hear nothing, no news is good news, but it's good to provide the opportunity.

Summary

Rehearsals are brilliant. They truly are the moment everything starts to piece together.

The most important element is to find a room the director is happy with that doesn't break your budget.

- Be abreast of what's going on, both through rehearsal reports, and simply by being around.
- Be there often enough to be present but not so often that you're in the way.
- Make sure the notes from the rehearsal reports are being actioned. This is most easily done at the weekly production meeting.
- Go to the first run you're invited to.

Enjoy this creatively exciting, and generally calm, period, the intensity is about to ramp up!

12

Into the theatre

Rehearsals finish, your first performance is days away and in between you have the small matter of the get-in, tech and dress rehearsals. This is the most intense period of the show. I love it and hate it.

I love that it's where the magic comes from. The designs come together and transform the show that you saw a few days ago in a bare rehearsal room.

It's also where stuff goes wrong. Your budget will be stretched to the limit. And stress levels will be highest. But your fabulous team will manage the best they can, ingeniously solving problems that arise. And you'll get through just fine.

Cheerleading skills fully engaged. Let's go.

The get-in

The get-in (or load-in) is when your set is assembled, your costumes and props arrive at the theatre, and the lights and speakers are hung in the grid.

The key variables are the scale of the set build, the quantity of lights and sound and the number of skilled people you're able to pay to help. Hopefully you will have your budget contingency still remaining as the get-in and tech is where any overspend is going to happen. This is where you will learn the value in having a good production manager.

The most likely holdup to starting the technical rehearsal on time is lighting. They need to rig (hang the lights in the grid), focus (point them in the right direction) and plot the lights, (enter into the computer system the correct collection of lights on at any one time) before tech can begin. Lighting designers may want a production electrician (Prod LX) or a lighting programmer to speed up the process. It will be slower if you don't have them.

As producer I check in on the get-in, but usually it runs smoothly. Bringing sweet treats makes me more popular. I discourage directors coming in; they add little value but plenty of stress. Often the get-in happens on a Monday, in which case, you might hire a rehearsal space for the day for the director to do another run-through with the cast, rather than be at the get-in.

If the get-in does run significantly behind, there should be constant communication between you, the director and the production manager about the best way to handle it. If you can pay more people to come help or pay the venue to do an overnight, that is almost certainly better than cancelling your first preview, or missing a dress rehearsal. Good usage for the contingency.

Part of the get-in involves showing the cast their dressing rooms. Dressing rooms vary. You should have seen them when you first saw the venue, and you should have let the cast know the situation when they were contracted. However, make sure you check they're clean, all the light bulbs are working and they are as inviting a place to be as possible. This should be the venue's responsibility, but it'll be you fielding the complaints.

Technical rehearsals

After the get-in comes tech. In tech you run through the whole show slowly, plotting light and sound cues into the stage manager's script, and testing all set, costumes and props. It is managed by the stage manager, with the DSM, designers and director in the auditorium. If you have only one stage manager, they will be in the auditorium and do their best to control proceedings on stage from there.

This rehearsal is not an opportunity for the director or actors to try new things. They've had weeks in the rehearsal room and have previews still to come. This is the one opportunity for the design and tech team to get the show right. Professional directors and actors know this. Many actors like tech rehearsals as it's an opportunity to cement the show in their minds, while the pressure is on everyone else.

As a producer you should be present, but not involved. I tend to sit in the bar; a colleague of mine likes to be at the back of the auditorium. Cheerleading is hopefully all you'll have to do. Some directors hold a meeting at the end of each session (morning/afternoon/evening) to plan the next one – you should be at these. Check that communication is happening, progress is being made and breaks are being taken!

Tech will probably overrun. It usually does. It can be stressful, and you need to keep tabs on just how behind it is running. Sometimes designers are being overly picky, sometimes directors, and sometimes there's just a hell of a lot to do. It is vital, however, that dress rehearsals and first previews are not compromised. It is better to fix small things during previews than to slow down tech.

Cancelling shows as a result of tech overruns is not acceptable, and should be an absolute last resort. And your first paying audience should feel comfortable that there has been a dress rehearsal in advance. I've never missed either a dress rehearsal or first preview, so it is possible. Whatever your director is telling you.

In the unlikely possibility you end up ahead on the schedule – consider another dress rehearsal. If you can manage two, the first preview will be stronger for it.

Dress rehearsal

The dress rehearsal is the first opportunity to see the show come together. It should be treated by everyone as if it was a full performance, no breaks, no stopping. If any lines are forgotten the actors should just carry on, or be prompted by stage management as per any other performance.

It's vital that you watch the dress rehearsal. It's your first look at your show as a whole and it's thrilling. While watching, consider it from an audience perspective. What are the sight-lines like? How long is it? Are the seats uncomfortable? All the things you'd rather know before an audience member tells you. Having someone from the venue watch (ideally the artistic director) is useful to get another perspective.

Often, the dress rehearsal happens on the afternoon before the first preview performance. Sometimes the morning has been used to finish off the tech. All of this makes for a long, stressful day, in particular for the actors and stage management. Stay calm, encourage the director to cut whatever corners are necessary and tell everyone what a fantastic job they're doing.

After first preview, I buy a round of drinks to say thank you for people's hard work. Adrenalin will be high and your team will want to decompress. Don't forget stage management who will be the last people into the bar!

Previews

Previews are full performances to a paying audience that happen before press night. They're something that happen on every show. You charge slightly less for the ticket, to reflect the fact that the show isn't completely ready yet.

Previews are a great time to make tweaks and changes, using nightly audience reaction in order to perfect the show. You use the daytime each day to work on different sections of the show, and perfect the designs. You will be amazed how much the show changes through previews. The real work starts the moment the first preview ends.

Your first preview will be incredibly exciting. Theatre is nothing without an audience, and now you have your first. They're usually friendly, as friends and family often book to see the first show. You will see the actors come alive as they have a living breathing audience to react to what they're doing on stage. Some bits will exceed your expectations, other bits will fall flat. But this, finally, is a real response to your show.

There's an old phrase that you can see who the producer is in the audience as they're the person watching the audience, not the show. I certainly spend far more time watching the audience than the show once I get in there. You can feel how people are enjoying it, when or where they're laughing, when they're fidgeting and when they're engrossed. Remember it, note it down and help the director to make the show better before the press come in.

Immediately after a preview a director will sit down with everyone apart from the cast and give their 'tech notes' on what needs changing the following day. The production manager will then organize a schedule.

Avoid changes between the last preview and press night for the actors' sake. For actors to give their best performances on press night they need to feel comfortable. Changes during previews, particularly 'trying stuff out'-type changes, make them uncomfortable, especially the first time they try. As such, the day of the last preview is the last chance for the director to tweak, and then the day of press night should be free for rest and running lines, if necessary.

Creative feedback

An underrated part of a producer's role is to provide creative feedback to the director. Obviously, if you are the director or an actor in the show, this is not possible. But if you are just a producer, then it's something you should be doing.

The first run you watch in the rehearsal room is the only time that the show will feel 'new' to you. It's the closest you will get to the audience's experience. After that run, you know what's coming, so your experience will never be the same.

I take detailed notes about how I feel watching it. The characters and sections that interest and excite me, what's funny and where I think they're missing the gag and, crucially, is the storytelling clear? I then sit with the director and talk-through my thoughts.

Most directors consider this to be valuable. They have seen everything so many times they're eager for a trusted outside perspective. Notes are exclusively to *help* the director. They are not commands, they are discussion points. You have to trust your director to deliver the show as best they can, and you are there as a resource to be mined. I do insist that we have the conversation, however, as I may have spotted something they haven't thought about. Only bad directors don't want feedback.

Point out problems, don't offer solutions. The director knows better than you how the show is constructed, and while you will be correct that Scene 5 is not landing right, the director will know that it's because a piece of information in Scene 2 is being missed. It's a remarkably hard lesson to learn, but every time I give notes, it confirms that my solutions are rubbish. Just identify problems. Theatre is a team effort and the key is to get it right, not to worry about whose vision it came from.

Press night

Press night is the most important night of the run. Your limited marketing budget means you need the reach that good reviews bring.

I will talk more about the critic side of press night later when discussing press and marketing. From a company perspective there will be a lot of nerves, excitement and anticipation of a party afterwards. This is the final night you will see the director and designers as their job is done. This is a positive. Actors will relax into their roles and cease to worry about regular director feedback, and stage management will take charge – always a good thing.

On press night itself, you should give every member of the team a pair of seats (if there's room) to allow them to bring a guest. I write a thank you card to *everyone* involved. It's important to mark the occasion, and it's your job to ensure everyone is acknowledged. Other producers go bigger with press night presents, all will be appreciated – the key is to say thank you.

After the performance try to find a way to offer something. It's hard when you have a tight budget, but even if it's a few bottles of wine to share, the gesture is appreciated. Stay at the venue bar if appropriate, or invite the company to bring their guests somewhere else.

Into the run

Once press night is done, your focus will switch to sales and marketing. However, there are a few things to be aware of.

I try to attend the production at least once a week. The actors love to have someone from the team in to check it's ok. You are attending (and watching) in pure cheerleader capacity. The director will come back to note the show at some point, chat to them if you have creative concerns, not to the actors directly. The fewer in the audience, the more regularly you should be there. If it's not going well, your team are going to require more support.

Being present regularly helps check that the stage manager doesn't have concerns they've been sitting on. They want to make your job as easy as possible, so may not feedback minor concerns. In person, they're more likely to tell you everything.

The venue should take responsibility for making sure the technical level of the show is maintained. If a light is not working the venue technical manager should change it. Your production manager should make sure this is going to happen before they leave.

Also:

- Make sure laundry is happening ok.
- Pay people promptly on the correct day. Agents (rightly) get angry if payment is late. Too many shows default on payments for them to be anything other than itchy.

It's probably understandable, but you'll soon learn that successful shows have far fewer problems than unsuccessful ones.

Show reports

You should get a show report from your stage manager for each performance. This will summarize errors in the performance, the audience size, the running time and anything else notable. These paint a picture for the creative team members who weren't there. You should expect problems flagged on the show report to be addressed by the team.

Cancelling shows

Occasionally having to cancel a show is an unfortunate reality where there aren't understudies. Your venue contract may seek to penalize you for it, and yet it's never your fault. Things happen, and people will do whatever they can to make sure the show goes on. Both occasions I've had to cancel a show the cast have begged me to do an extra matinee in order to make it up. They all understand the financial pressures, and care that the show does as well as it possibly can.

I'm lucky never to have had to cancel more than one performance. If you do, it's a horrible situation, and you must solve it as best you can. Alternative actors going on with the script is not uncommon, or the director could play a role, maybe even you could?! All have been done. The key is to make sure your communication with all parties is clear. The venue will be anxious as it reflects badly on them. Keep everyone in the loop and all will be ok.

After the run is over

After closing night, I always feel a sense of sadness and a sense of relief. Which is the stronger feeling depends on how well the show has gone.

Main responsibilities

- Chase remaining invoices, and the venue settlement. *Aim* to get the accounts signed off within six weeks. Read the venue settlement in detail. There are well-respected venues where I've found £1000s of inaccuracies. Never in my favour. Refer back to your venue contract. Look out for rogue marketing charges that they said they'd cover months ago when you agreed on the deal.
- Ensure your PR sends over a 'press pack'. A record of all the press for the run.
- Follow up with anyone that saw it regarding the future life of the show.
- Talk to your accountant about the possibility of applying for Theatre Tax Relief.
- Sleep.

Summary

Good producers and general managers are ahead of everyone else on the show. They know when it's going well and step back, and when anxiety is growing, step in.

Managing people is a skill. Managing artists is harder. Remember, they all want to do the best possible job to make something great. If someone is being difficult, try to find out what they're insecure about and what you can do to ease that.

- Support your director through tech week, it's a stressful time.
- Watch the dress rehearsal and previews and give the director your notes.
- Watch the show regularly. Particularly if the show is not doing that well. Stay positive. You're in charge; your positivity will rub off on everyone.
- Tell the company they're amazing. All the time. Because they are.
- Say thank you.

INTERVIEW WITH PRODUCTION MANAGER HEATHER DOOLE

Heather is an experienced production manager who has built her career from the smallest theatres to the National Theatre and West End. She and I worked together successfully a number of times; her significant abilities and calm positive demeanour got us through many a tricky tech.

Tim Johanson I'm aware that some of my questions might perhaps hark back a few years.

Heather Doole First principles from the fringe are the most important thing. They apply everywhere and if you can apply them well elsewhere, then life becomes a lot easier.

TJ So what are your fringe first principles?

HD Working out capacity and being honest.

TJ Capacity as in your capacity?

HD Your personal capacity, but also capacity of the budget, the schedule, the venue. And then being really honest about that really quickly.

And then also not being afraid to try and bodge it. Never be afraid to go, 'Well that should cost £20,000, but I've got a hose and some guttering, let's see what happens'.

TJ And that applies . . .

HD That applies everywhere. It applies here at the National, it applies in the West End.

TJ Why did you work on the fringe in the first place?

HD I fell into it. I used to be a producer for a small theatre company and I also did stage management. I had no idea what a production manager was and I didn't see the point of them when people explained it, because I was doing it all.

And then I was talking to somebody saying, 'I'm planning on leaving my job. I don't know what to do'. He was a production manager and everything he was describing were the bits of producing I liked. And I didn't realize were a separate job.

And he put me forward for a few things. And going and working in all of the small theatres was a great way to learn because you're by yourself and you have to solve all of the problems.

TJ And working at that scale was fun?

HD So much fun. There's something freeing about being in the Finborough at midnight and knowing that there's pressure because you've got to solve this problem, but that there's no wrong answer.

TJ What are the drawbacks to working at the smaller scale?

HD It's really lonely. You're the only person who can solve this problem. You're the one who has to decide whether or not something

is realistic. And once you've said it's realistic, it's up to you to deliver that.

But when the producer-production manager relationship really works, and when I've always felt lucky, is when I've had a producer that can tell I'm having a bad day, when I can say 'this is a disaster and I don't know how to fix it'. And I know that they trust me enough that I will fix it but just have a problem right now. If you're lucky, the producer is the person that you have that relationship with at the small scale.

TJ   Would you go to a director with an issue?

HD   Never the director because they're somebody that you need to hold. You need to make sure that the director isn't worried about these things that you're doing. It's never helpful for them to know that you are worried, in my experience.

TJ   Were there patterns to shows that went well?

HD   The ones that had a lot more time in advance. If you can get set design ideas early, you've got longer to solve the problems.

Mostly it's about personalities. Most of the shows that have gone well are when you have that exact set of the people who get on well and who work in a similar fashion, who are collaborative and who are sensitive to each other's needs.

TJ   If you could choose between having enough time or enough money, do you have a preference?

HD   Time. They are pretty comparable. To an extent you can buy more time. Because you can buy more people. You can buy overnight calls. But that's really at the crunch point. And if you've got more time, you can solve problems in advance. You can source things for free. You can make sure that everybody knows exactly where they stand before you go into tech.

TJ   Are there patterns to shows that were harder, or more stressful, or the results you were less pleased with?

HD   There are two things. It comes back to time again, but if there is a member of a team who is not able to engage until later, if people haven't been able to pay attention and have been signing things off through the process, and then at the last minute, realize they haven't thought about it enough or have agreed to something and then realized it's not what they want. That has been the major thing.

And the other thing has been an unwillingness to compromise. Whether that's the designer, or the director or one of the performers. And there have been things that have been difficult to deliver, or impossible to deliver that have been insisted on. And you wind up wasting a lot of time trying to deliver that thing and everything else gets neglected. So even if you do end up achieving it, you maybe don't achieve it to the highest standard or you achieve that and you achieve nothing else.

TJ   Taking yourself back to the smaller theatre days . . . how many shows were you doing a year?

HD   Somewhere between a dozen and twenty. The kind of fees that you get means that's how much work you need to do in order to make a reasonable living.

TJ   What are the consequences of doing that many?

HD   It means that you have less time for everyone. Production management fundamentally doesn't work as a job because you've got unavoidable points where you absolutely have to be there, that clash for two different shows all the time.

So it means that you might be in third preview and you think you'll definitely be able to slip out and do a white card [pre-model box version of the set] somewhere else. But actually when it comes to third preview, your lighting wall has failed the previous night. And that whole day is spent fixing that. And you're constantly torn in two. It means that you do always feel you're letting somebody down. And it means that things get missed and things aren't ever quite as good as you'd hope they would be on each show.

But it never stops being true. When you work on bigger shows those timelines are longer, but those deadlines still clash.

TJ   What's the key to a successful tech period?

HD   Preparation and consideration of other people.

Having everybody knowing exactly what you're going to do when you go in. I love it when stage managers create breakdowns of where we need to get to in each section. And then you do some form of a pre-tech meeting with the creative team, so everyone gets on the same page.

TJ   And the key to a successful get-in? Presuming there's not enough time . . .

HD   There's never enough time. There's never enough time and there's never enough money and it doesn't matter how much time and how much money there is, there's never enough because the show just expands.

So it's almost the same answer as for the tech. It's preparation and careful scheduling.

You have to plan everything up to the moment that you get in the theatre. And then you have to be prepared to throw that away at a second's notice. Having as much understanding as possible, so that when things do go wrong, you're prepared.

TJ   I wouldn't do your job for anything.

HD   It's the best job in the world. It's so exciting. Particularly that moment in tech, if you have that full knowledge, being able to slot everything back together and go, this should waste a day. It's not wasting a day. It's wasting us half a day.

Exciting.

TJ How much do you end up doing with shows once they're open?

HD Hardly anything as a general rule. If things go wrong, you'll probably come in. But by that point, you're onto another show. So it gets a lot harder. And then it becomes about the relationship with stage management. How you can support stage management to solve the problems and work with the venue.

TJ What are the hallmarks of a good production manager–producer relationship?

HD Honesty in both directions.

One of my least favourite things that happens with producers, and it happens all the time, and I understand why, because everyone likes to be the hero, but when I've been working hard to keep it in budget, you keep saying, 'Absolutely no, we can't have that paint call. There's no more money for that paint call. We've got to accept that this is what it is.' And then the designer calls the producer, and the producer goes, 'Absolutely, of course you can have another paint call.'

It's so undermining, because it means that next time your designer will never trust a no from you. They will always keep going back to the producer.

The opposite of that is the hallmark of a good relationship.

TJ Not being undermined.

HD Not being undermined. I don't think producers realize that they're doing it because it is lovely to be able to say yes to people.

One of my favourite interactions with a producer was, I'd hit a problem with a director who was upset about replacing something. But the thing that he wanted to replace it with didn't exist, which he took quite personally. And after we'd had that conversation, I went to the producer and said, 'Either you're going to get a lot of complaints about me in the next week, or it's going to get expensive.'

And they looked at their spreadsheet and got out their calculator and said, 'You can spend up to this much to make this problem go away'. So they didn't say to the director, 'Yes, of course you can have this impossible thing'. They were like, 'I don't mind getting complaints about you. Here's how much money you've got. Go and please make these problems go away.'

And that level of trust, I really appreciated.

Part II – Conclusion

The management of the show can feel like the main body of producing. Managing the company, managing the budget, managing rehearsals, managing the first week in the theatre and managing your smash hit.

There's a lot of technical stuff (company set-up, contracts, accountancy), but you can get help with all that. The key is to be organized, get stuff done and out of the way (particularly recruitment, you can't do this too early) and allow yourself time to focus on the fun bits – casting, rehearsals, filming videos and running photo shoots.

- Work out who your director is first. Everything else begins with them.
- Nobody else is essential on a show. Probably you need three designers, but there are no wrong answers.
- Trust your team. If you don't, there's no point having them. They're all bringing specialist knowledge.
- A casting director's lists are invaluable.
- If you're going to employ a general manager, get someone who's excited about the show. It's just administration, so they can learn the expertise, but enthusiasm can't be learned.
- Set up a company to protect yourself.
- Get contracts done early.
- Rehearsals are great. Be around them but not in them.
- During tech week, be sure to breathe. You and everyone else will get through it. Be the best cheerleader you can be.
- Enjoy the run, this is what you've been working for.

So, we've got through the management of the show. That's it isn't it? That's what producing is? Build it and they will come!

No. Sorry. Not a chance. This is where the hard work begins . . .

Gulp.

PART III

Selling your show

If a tree falls in a forest and there's no one there to hear it, does it make a sound? If you make a show and there's no audience, is it theatre?

Maybe it is. But it's a lot better with an audience, and that means you're going to have to sell some tickets

Selling tickets is an alchemy that every producer in the world is trying to master.

What is it that makes an audience member buy a ticket for a particular show?

Do they like the writer? Do they like the actor or the theatre? The original film? All of the above? Almost certainly. But there are shows that ticked all of those boxes that have flopped in a big way.

Answering this question will go a long way to establishing the success of your show. I will give you my theories and approaches, but there isn't one right answer. If there were, every theatre would be full every night.

There are endless strands to talk about with regards to selling your show. Your limited budget simplifies things slightly. So how to do it? Through press, marketing and sales.

Press (or PR) is journalists featuring your show in their publications. Alongside newspapers, this includes blogs, radio, TV, podcasts and crucially the critics. None of this costs you anything (apart from probably a press rep – more on them shortly), but you don't control the content.

Marketing is any media in which you control the content, and would expect to pay for – adverts, emails, posters, flyers, content (photos/videos) and social media. It's important to understand the distinction between PR and marketing as, if you are getting help, they are almost always done by different people.

Generally, press and marketing is as far as producers get. They are well-established methods for getting word of the show out. But there should also be a clear third plan, for sales. This will often come under a marketing plan, but I find it useful to draw a distinction between them.

These three plans interact with one another, with you at the centre. It's up to you to work out what's the best use of your time and your budget, and it's up to you to drive each of them. We're going to look at a theoretical schedule to help.

Remember, everything has the same goal of selling a ticket. As you read the next sections and think about your show, keep that in mind. Who is going to be affected by the activity you're planning? And will it help sell tickets?

Word of mouth

Before we get into the detail, it's important we talk about word of mouth. Of the last five shows you went to, I'll wager that four out of five, *at least*, were because someone you know told you about it. You may have seen the ads, read the articles and reviews, but it's when your friend tells you it's brilliant that you buy a ticket.

Word of mouth is, *by miles*, the most important factor in selling tickets. It relies on two things.

- The show is good. No one tells their friends to see something bad. And nothing in sales or marketing can cover up a bad show.
- You have enough people there in the first place in order to start the word of mouth. If there's barely anyone watching it to begin with, there's no one to pass on the good news about a great show.

The quality of the show is outside of the realm of the press and marketing campaigns. That's on you and your creative team. So, this part is all about that second point.

How do you get people there, *before* they know it's any good? Because if you get enough people there at the beginning, and it *is* a good show, then you'll have a hit.

13

Press

Until you're working at a significant scale, the single most important thing to spend money on is a press rep (see sales section for most important thing to do, full stop!). If you get the press right on your show, you can get coverage that would cost you a small fortune to pay for. I have mentioned previously the double-page article in The Guardian supplement that cost me nothing. The show was about Barack Obama just before his 2012 election and the right journalist thought that was interesting.

Starting press early

There is significant overlap between what an audience is interested in, and what the press are interested in. It should be on your mind from when you're deciding what to produce in the first place. Not only will you make your press rep's job easier by having something to say, you will also be presenting something that the audience will be intrigued by.

In order to establish what the press might write about, you must understand your show. Put yourself in a journalist's shoes. What is it about your show that is newsworthy? Is it a well-known writer, a current affairs piece or a new take on a known historical event?

If you don't think it has strong enough appeal by itself, are there similar shows happening in the same area that you could pitch together? Three new plays by young female writers? Could it be something about the venue you're going to? Is there a ten-/fifteen-/twenty-year anniversary?

If the answer is no to all of these, then you end up trying to create appeal with casting. As we've touched on, that's not easy. But it is the way to turn any show into a show the press wants to talk about.

Press representative

To best achieve strong press coverage, you should hire a press rep. They will have the right contacts to 'pitch' the show quickly and easily and will stand you in the best stead for attracting critics.

Given the importance of press, I would spend up to 50 per cent of my marketing/sales/press budget on the right person. Seriously. It's hard to generate a return on marketing spend with limited budgets, and press can allow you to stand out.

It can feel like a lot of money for an individual, particularly as it may well be equivalent to, or more than, the director. The difference is they are solely doing it for the money. So, the good ones won't do it if the money isn't there.

It's hard to evaluate press reps. Often press coverage is generated through contacts of whole teams, so it's not entirely straightforward what the rep themselves delivered.

Try to find people who've worked with the various reps. And try to make it more than one person you talk to. People are quick to blame the rep if the show isn't getting coverage. Knowing whether it's the rep or the show itself is key in this evaluation.

Your press rep should attempt to deliver two things:

- Feature coverage in advance of press night about the show
- Good attendance from critics at the show

Critics coming to the show is the most important, and as such what many reps focus on. However, a good rep should deliver *some* sort of feature coverage in advance of the show. It probably won't be an article in the Guardian, but local radio, online interviews or an opportunity to contribute to a prominent blog are all achievable.

Press release

In order to communicate with the press, you are going to need a press release. This is the way to announce your show, casting or anything else newsworthy.

A press release is a (maximum) two-page document that should read like a newspaper article, to the extent that it could be copied and pasted directly as an article. This happens more often than you'd expect. On every show I've done I have seen my press release written word for word somewhere online.

Major West End shows may send five-plus press releases with information before the show opens – that the show is happening, the ticket-on-sale date, the principal casting, secondary casting, creative team etc. Each one of these is calculated to get coverage in the press.

If you're not working on a big show with a big name, you are likely to send one or two releases. Either, simply one with all of the information you have. Or, one announcing the show and one with casting. Often, casting happens well after you want to announce the show, in which case, two releases is standard. Sending more risks fatiguing journalists' interest in your show on non-newsworthy material.

The language of a press release should be purely factual. This is in contrast to marketing copy (more on that later). It needs to present the most interesting facts to journalists, in as impactful a way as possible. No flowery language unless it's a quote. Do not describe your show as 'hilarious', or 'interesting', in a press release, unless you are quoting something someone else has said. If you write that your show is hilarious, a journalist's reaction is, 'Says who?' If you write that Stephen Fry called the script 'hilarious', you are merely stating a fact. The journalist's reaction is 'ok, that's interesting'. It's a subtle, but important difference.

With this in mind, most press releases have a quote from the most prominent person involved. It might be you, it might be the director or it might be the artistic director of the theatre. They can say what they like about the show, as it's a quote. If journalists don't like it, they won't use it. If in doubt, return to the idea that it should read like a newspaper article.

There should be a section at the end called Notes to Editors. This is information that will appear alongside your article, including the venue, dates, prices and box office information. It comes after the 'newspaper article' section of the release.

Sending the show announcement is an important moment in a campaign, even if you don't get huge coverage from it. Once the initial release is sent, the starting gun on the show is fired. You, your team and your rep can start to talk about the show.

Feature coverage

Feature coverage is positive coverage about your production, usually in advance of opening. It is anything you read in the press about a show that is not a review. It's often an interview with someone involved.

I'd always expect coverage from theatre-specific media – websites, radio, maybe a podcast. Coverage in the major publications is obviously desirable, but can be hard to deliver. Particularly as your rep will have a number of shows they're pitching every time they talk to a journalist. This is frustrating, but it is a reality.

I have more often succeeded with larger feature coverage when it's been me or someone on the creative team who has generated it. *You* will always be the best person at selling your show. If you meet a journalist at a party, or a friend of a friend works for a local radio station, use the contact as best you can. Don't just wait for your rep (but do let them know).

Any cast interviews you do secure will happen during the rehearsal and tech periods. The exact times the director needs the actors most. The director has to understand the cast need releasing to do these. As usual communication is key.

There is a *tiny* chance a particular actor might have their own press rep or be expecting PR fees for doing interviews, though I've never experienced either situation. If you do, work with their rep as best you can, they may have access to different journalists. PR fees, however, are not appropriate. The actor should understand the scale and limitations of what they've signed up for (and almost certainly will, it'll be their team who are pushing for more).

Critics

The most important part of the press, sales and marketing campaign is ensuring critics come. Good reviews give the show a sales boost, give the company a lift that carries you through the run and gives you and your show the profile you need. Getting critics to come is your rep's most important responsibility.

Only the biggest openings get a full house of critics. For smaller-scale shows there is no way that will happen. It may be that a single 'established' critic is the best-case scenario. However, there are tons of blogs, websites and YouTube critics that can give a critical assessment of your show.

The majority of critics will come on press night. It's likely that your rep will ask if they can invite critics during previews. A show improves greatly during previews. Having critics come to see it while it's still improving is dangerous: no review is better than a bad one. Equally, if it's the only time the major critics can come, is it worth the risk? It's a balance.

Discuss this with your director. They will understand the dilemma. However, they will be understandably annoyed to see someone scribbling before press night if they don't know in advance.

Critics follow one another to good shows. Don't despair if you don't have the publications you want on press night. The right blog can lead to the right WhatsOnStage or The Stage review, which may even lead to The Guardian or The Times coming – keep pushing throughout the run. Even a reviewer in on your last night may give you the review you need for the future life of the show.

Dressing the house

On press night some people get worried about who is sat where. Your rep will be one of them. Giving critics the best sense makes good sense to their potential enjoyment of the show.

Depending on how vigilant your rep has been, they might have fifty or more tickets allocated to press. I would warn against their being more than 30–40 per cent of the audience. Some critics make for great audience members, but many don't. It's vital to have some general public in there as well (even if they're your friends), who will enjoy the show without a critical eye.

The worst audience members are the creative and production team, as they've seen the show many times before. Don't put them in the middle of the audience, particularly if your show is funny.

Press photocall

A press photocall is an opportunity for photographers associated with the national papers to take photos of the show. It typically takes place on press night or the day before. While many publications will just use photos you've had taken, major papers sometimes want their own image.

For the photocall, the actors and stage management run two or three scenes that you and the director have decided on. Look for the most dynamic, active scenes, avoiding any key visual spoilers. These will be in full costumes, make up and props. You need to have someone present who can adjust the lighting. Photographers always want more light than is in the show. Don't let anyone be precious about this; these photographers know what they're doing.

Once they've seen each scene for the first time, the photographers will direct what they want. Don't worry about artistic integrity at this point; if they want you to change things, this is all about getting a good photo.

It's lovely to have a photocall, as it usually means the biggest critics are coming to review. However, it's pretty common to schedule one and no one wants to come. Don't worry; it's far more usual not to have one. Your rep will make sure it's advertised and be in charge of who's coming.

DIY press

For many shows the amount of money you need to splash on a rep is too much. So here are additional tips for DIY press.

- Prepare a press release that looks professional and is no longer than two pages in total. Pay attention to punctuation and grammar.
- Make a concise list of journalists you're going to contact, work out whether you can find their email address, the arts desk email address or contact them on social media.
- When you're ready to launch, contact journalists with a brief cover explanation of your show and attach the release.

- Put the most newsworthy element in the subject of the email – 95 per cent won't get further than that. For example, 'Helen Mirren makes fringe debut'.
- Write to journalists with specific reasons why they personally might be interested in your show based on areas they've shown interest in the past, or their appreciation of someone involved. Better to do ten approaches well, than a hundred generically.
- Be realistic, most won't have time to reply.
- Be polite (*always*).
- Don't be a snob – the smallest blog is better than nothing.

Summary

Press is the way that small shows compete with large ones. It's free, and with the right story and approach, you can be sitting alongside the biggest shows. And whoever you are, you're going to want critics to come and see it.

- Think about the press angles at every stage of producing your show.
- If you possibly can, pay for a press rep, as long as you have a good reference for them.
- Push them, but trust them. Keep them onside.

If you're doing it yourself,

- Draft a press release that reads like a newspaper article.
- Target a few journalists and write personal emails.
- Don't give up if critics don't come to press night, keep going throughout the run.

Thinking about press is key to your whole experience of making a show. It's not about press defining your show, it's too much of an alchemy for that, but if you're thinking about it throughout, you will be prepared when your rep asks you, 'What can I sell about this show?'

INTERVIEW WITH PRESS REP CHLOÉ NELKIN, FOUNDER OF CHLOÉ NELKIN CONSULTING

Chloé is a press representative with over ten years' experience, and has probably worked at a wider variety of venues than anyone else in the UK, from small fringe venues to the West End and on tour. She is also one of the most in-demand Edinburgh Fringe reps.

Tim Johanson What is it that you're looking for when somebody comes to you with a show?

Chloé Nelkin Something that sounds exciting from the first two or three lines of reading their email. If the email from them describing their own show is boring, it's hard work to want to progress to the script and then be excited on their behalf. If the producer can't make it sound exciting . . .

TJ Are you looking at it from a PR angle at that point?

CN Well, in a sense. But, first of all, they have to excite me. As soon as they excite me, then my brain starts going 'ooh ok, well we could talk to so and so about that'.

TJ What percentages of pitches do you take on?

CN 50:50. Fewer for Edinburgh. For Edinburgh last year we took about 15 per cent to 20 per cent of the shows that approached us. A lot of people forget that they need PR until a month before opening so we have to just turn them down on that basis.

TJ When do you want to be approached about a show? Is it as much time as possible?

CN For an Off-West End show, the campaign begins about two months before opening and we'd love to know four to six months out, as soon as they know they're doing a show. Unless there is someone mega famous in it, in which case announce whenever you can and sell as many tickets as possible.

For Edinburgh, the campaigns begin in March. We're already over half-full by December, but I try to keep slots open for a little while after that.

TJ Do you have a preferred way for people to approach you?

CN We like it when people email us with all of the information. The most annoying thing is when people tell us there's a show happening at X venue, and do we want to work on it? No, we don't know what your show is. The most helpful way is to get in touch with the script, the synopsis, the dates, the venue – everything straightaway. That way we have all the information and can take a couple of days to think about it.

TJ   What can a producer do to make your life as easy as possible?

CN   Provide the information they've been asked for. For a PR to do their job we have to have been given the information. We can read the script and come up with the angles and know how we'd like to sell the show but, unless you have an inkling as to how the producer thinks their show should be sold, you're on completely different pages to begin with.

    We send a theatre check list now, which is everything we need. Copy, basic details and a stream of consciousness from the director or writer to help us understand the show in their words. Where's everyone from in the cast? Does anyone know any press? What are your social media handles? My biggest bugbear is its coming back half completed. Because then we get halfway through the campaign and the producer wonders why we didn't do any regional-specific PR. Well, you didn't tell us that was relevant.

TJ   Once the campaign is going, what do you then want from the producer?

CN   Responsiveness. I would like timely replies. Once you've given me all of the information, I just need you to reply to emails.

    Also. Be grateful to your PR. We don't need patting on the back all the time but . . . We have a client at the moment where we've landed various national features, the campaign couldn't be going better. Her tickets aren't selling, but that's not what PR always does. There's not been a single 'thank you' or 'please' once in three months. It's demoralizing. It's not hard, it's just manners.

TJ   No one's making much money in theatre. All we can do is be nice to one another.

    In terms of features versus critics – how do you weight their importance?

CN   It's impossible. You can't. Literally can't. In terms of analysis, PR doesn't equate to sales. You can't say, 'I got that double spread in the Sunday Times this weekend, and so I sold tickets'. You hope it does, but we've had instances where we've had that spread and we've sold out, and also where we sold five tickets. PR is hard to analyse.

    It depends on the show, even on the fringe, if you have a show with a famous person, we should be able to get them on breakfast television, we should be able to get that huge interview. On the smaller show without that, the unfortunate reality is you're not often going to get that big national coverage.

TJ   Taking that smaller show. The critics become everything?

CN   Yes. Critics are important. But if you've had a show with enough preview coverage, even small, you can sell a show without a national critic. If you rely on a national critic to sell a show, and they turn up and give you two stars, then you're screwed if that's what you've been riding on. It's about maintaining that visibility through the press in advance, through things like small Q&As and radio interviews, as well as trying to get the bigger stuff, and then you try to get the national critics as well.

TJ   What place do influencers play in a campaign?

CN   It really depends on the campaign and the goals but we work closely with influencers – although typically this is on our family or West End shows. Influencers have huge reach and as corny as it sounds they lend their influence when they support a project. They do sit on the line between marketing and PR, so, as with any journalist, for us it's important we build the relationships with them. They need to know if they're coming to one of our shows they're going to have a fun night. And if they have a fun night, they post stories and their followers start flocking.

TJ   Theoretically, what does success looks like for the hardest show you've ever worked on?

CN   Success should be ten to fifteen people reviewing press night, a local radio slot, a handful of Q&A/features in advance and a couple of round-ups.

   Unless you get no coverage, I genuinely don't consider a PR campaign to have failed. You can't quantify PR. I can't say that five hours' work will mean five features. We sometimes work solidly for a month, and you're pulling out your hair thinking why is no one biting on this, when we think it's incredible. We've had a show like that recently – it did alright, I'd have liked more press, it deserved more press, but I sure as hell know we tried to get it more press.

TJ   Let's talk about press night. How important is it?

CN   Important and not important. Important in that you have to do it, it's tradition, the majority of press come. But, it's vital for producers to remember that because critics haven't come on press night, it doesn't mean they're not going to come.

   My advice is to have press night as early as you can (when the show is ready) and know the PR will keep on pushing for critics to come. They'll come when they want to. Press night isn't gospel.

TJ   What is it that the critics will always come and see?

CN   Casting.

TJ   Ok, taking that as read. What next? Venue?

CN   No. Topicality helps but not if it's the same as everyone else. You have to find your niche. Journalists have the same thing sold to them all day every day.

TJ   In terms of topicality, is there a benefit to its being newsworthy?

CN   That helps a lot because you're pitching to the news desk not the arts desk. That's often my dream as a PR, not to have to pitch to the arts editor. The arts desk does not have the time to process all they're pitched. As soon as you can pitch to the family pages, the news desk, the women's sections, you stand a much better chance.

TJ   Anything particular from after press night? I tend to speak to you a lot less!

CN   If the reviews are bad, the PR gets stuck. I can pitch and re-pitch, but fundamentally everyone's read it's a two-star show. That's when marketing needs to take over.

TJ   How does Edinburgh differ?

CN   Completely. We start the campaigns six months before, rather than two. We pitch to different press, different blogs. And we have to be more persistent. If you think the competition in London is high, get to Edinburgh and it's a whole another level. We push and push and push in a way that I never would in London.

TJ   Journalists are more prepared for that?

CN   Yes, absolutely.

TJ   Does that make a press rep all the more important in Edinburgh?

CN   I don't think you can survive in Edinburgh without a press rep. It's so tough and competitive.

TJ   Does the venue make a big difference?

CN   Huge. It has to, just logistically. For the amount we do in Edinburgh we physically can't be, or liaise with that many venues all at once. Because of this, we will now only work with Pleasance, Underbelly, Assembly, Gilded Balloon, Summerhall and the Traverse. I've got to filter somehow.

TJ   Where does money come into it?

CN   I now tell people the fee before I'll engage with it. I used to read scripts and be excited and then discover they only have £500. We just can't do shows for that. Also, to an extent you get what you pay for. Anyone who's charging £500, you're probably getting a £500 service.

TJ   If someone couldn't afford you, what's the best thing they could do with whatever they might have?

CN   Do it themselves. Think carefully about the approaches they're making. 'I'm writing to you as I know you're really interested by dementia as a topic', or 'you happen to be best friends with the actor in my play'. It's better to email ten organizations like that than 100 people when you don't know what you're doing. Spend the time working out why you want to write to those ten people and think carefully about your approach.

Journalists respond well to your making their life easy. You have to give them the story rather than just giving them a press release and saying 'it's really good'. You have to say, 'I think this should go in your page five column and this is the story'. They're overworked and often underpaid.

TJ Sounds like if someone can't afford a press rep, they should keep their £500 in their pocket and spend it on something else?

CN Absolutely.

14

Marketing

People talk a lot about marketing. In all of life. Including in theatre. What it means is often misunderstood – including by me. Wikipedia says it's 'the study and management of exchange relationships'. So clear as mud.

For the purposes of this book, I'm going to define it as activity that helps sell your show, that you control (not press), but is likely to cost you money upfront (not sales).

I'm going to break it down into three sections: brand, content and distribution. Content is the most important of these. But the first thing you'll do is create a brand. So, we'll start there.

The best piece of marketing advice I've been given is that whatever you do, it must be *impactful*. One thing done well that makes an impact is worth ten done in passing that no one notices.

Before we get into it, a word on marketing agencies.

Marketing agencies

Marketing agencies are big in the West End. No one will market a show without them. They are marketing specialists who manage an entire marketing campaign for a producer. I could write a lot about them at the smaller scale, but what it all boils down to is:

I have never experienced, or heard about, a successful collaboration with a full-service marketing agency at the small scale. Ever.

I'm not going to make myself popular by saying that. But there is not enough money in your budget for them to justify taking on the project, *and* to then do a good job. They may take on the project in order to build a relationship with an emerging producer, but they have nothing at stake. When push comes to shove, they will prioritize their bill-paying shows.

Do it yourself. All the best marketing campaigns I've seen have been led by the producer. That's not to say you shouldn't bring someone in to help you, but own the responsibility to sell tickets rather than delegating elsewhere. That pressure will help you do an even better job.

Brand

Brand is another word we hear a lot. Coca Cola's brand has been established for 100 years. Tightly controlled by the company, it's the key to its getting global recognition by consumers.

The first real theatre brand was *Cats*. Someone clever had the idea to strip everything away from the poster apart from the famous eyes. It was simple, clean and distinguished it from every other show. Immediately *Cats* ceased to be 'that show that's on at the New London Theatre', and became a brand. Now almost forty years on, like Coca Cola or McDonalds, it remains iconic worldwide.

But brand is not just a poster image. These days it's across all platforms. It's still about distinguishing yourself from the competition, but now includes your social media voice, the tone and style of your content and even how you conduct your business. A wonderful theatre example of a brand working across platforms is the Mischief Theatre set of farces that began with *The Play That Goes Wrong*. In the show everything goes wrong, so their marketing is littered with mistakes – text upside down, backwards, words missing, the wrong messaging – all in the service of establishing exactly the type of show you are going to see.

You won't have anything like those resources but it's worth understanding how brand works. For you it may begin and end with the image for the show, but that image must be distinctive, authentic to your show, and you should use it as a starting point to create the brand voice you can take onto your social media or in content creation.

Publicity image

Your publicity image is the first thing you'll create. It's the core image from which everything derives. Along with your copy, this is what you're going to need to go on sale. Often, you'll create it before even the creative team are in place.

Like everything else, there are cheaper and more expensive ways to do it. I have worked with the same graphic designer for years, and will describe our working method, but if you can achieve the same output a different way, then that's great, too.

You already know your show. So, when you first speak to a graphic designer you should have a good idea of the tone you'd like the image to send out. Initially I keep these thoughts to myself, and first see what my designer thinks of the script (beware the designer who doesn't read the script). We then have a discussion on the direction to take. Often, we agree immediately and I'm content to let her have a stab, or sometimes we need to throw example images back and forth in order to get a feel for what we want. She is much better at it than me, so I almost always defer to her.

Some quick tips on working with a graphic designer:

- Be careful how you give notes – they're a professional. 'Can we move that text up a bit' is a bad note, they'll have it where it is for a reason. 'The title isn't jumping out at me enough' is better. Offer problems not solutions and allow their talent to deliver results. Every single time I've got this wrong, and given a detailed note, I've made it worse. You're working with them for their talent.

- Only 25 per cent of the job is done when you agree on the logo/image. Much of the graphic designer's job is resizing the image for social media, venue brochures, poster, flyer, adverts, programme . . . the list goes on.

  A friend who will design you an image is almost useless if they aren't able to do all the iterations. At least if you are calling in a favour, have them do versions of the image for social media and then give you all the layered artwork. You can work from that.

- I sometimes find this a worthwhile process even before the show is confirmed in a theatre. It helps me understand my show, how I'm going to pitch it to theatres/investors and how I'm going to sell it.

I'm wary of involving other members of the team. Too many opinions don't bode well for coherent design. You may want to get your director's thoughts, but bear in mind this is your territory not theirs, so they need to understand that if you disagree, then you're making the final call.

Title treatment

Much of your brand may come down to your title treatment. If your title does a lot to describe the show, *The Play That Goes Wrong*, then you might not need much else in your image. Your designer will lead on this. Many theatres have a house style, and your treatment will be in their style whether you like it or not.

Photos

If you need to use photos for your image, don't just default to having a photo shoot, they are expensive! There's stock imagery that you can pay a small license fee for that could work. Chat with your designer.

Copy

Along with your initial image you need marketing copy. This is the description of a show you see in any theatre listing. You will require a range of lengths, for use in different places – twenty, fifty and hundred words are common. In particular, these will also go anywhere else you're selling tickets, for example, a ticket agent, on your venue website and on any flyers.

Marketing copy reads like a sales pitch. Whereas your press release is completely fact based, here you can use more descriptive language.

Read twenty different copies for shows at different scales, and then just have a go. If I'm working with new writing, I often ask writers to have a go – they won't get it right, but they are the persons who understand the show best, so it provides a starting point.

- Be as succinct as possible.
- Don't be aloof – explain what it is the show is about. If it's a romcom, call it that. Don't be too clever.
- Include anything that helps your show stand out – 'Award-winning', '5 stars in the Guardian', 'starring Helen Mirren', and so on.
- Credit people who will help sell the show – not others. They'll get their recognition elsewhere.

Be careful listing the themes of your show in the copy, 'a damning indictment of the effect of 1980s British economic policy on the working classes'. It's more interesting to hear about the characters' journey – 'The son of a striking miner joins a ballet school and thrives against the odds'.

While you may be doing the show to highlight something about society, don't forget the audience wants a story – they read about society in the news. So set up the story in your copy.

Creative credits on marketing

This is often an area of contention, and is something we've touched on in buying the rights and contracting your creative team. Creatives (or more realistically, creatives' agents) *love* having their name on the marketing. But unless that name is going to sell tickets, it's destructive to the impact of that marketing.

Have a look at some static advertising, both for theatre and non-theatre. What do you find most impactful? The answer is likely to be with the *least* text. The ideal for all imagery should be to have just the title (or in the case of *Cats*, nothing . . .) and possibly a tag line. You'll probably have to have the writers (though do not agree to their names being a per cent of the size of the title, it's a pain for the graphic designer), the dates and the name or logo of the theatre (but not both).

Nothing else.

When was the last time you wrote down the web address, phone number or anything else from a poster? Never. You remember the name and Google it. So will everyone else. Your company logo isn't important. The list of producers – totally unimportant. The purpose of your marketing is to sell tickets. Beginning, middle and end.

This does not mean you don't want to credit your team. List everyone on the theatre's website. Have a poster at the venue with a comprehensive listing of everyone involved: cast, creatives, stage management. If that's not possible, make sure there is, as a minimum, a cast sheet or, ideally, a programme with biographies.

If someone wants to know who's involved, they will use a search engine, or buy a programme. They won't look for an advert or on a poster. As long as you look after your team's credits appropriately, they will understand that your marketing image is exactly that.

Content

After a press rep, content is the most important place to spend your budget. You are trying to get as much coverage for as little money as possible. Press coverage allows that, and the right content can do the same thing. Why? Because if you get it right, then media outlets will distribute it for free. News organizations, online blogs, websites and social accounts are looking for content all day every day. It just has to be the best content it can be.

What do I mean by content? Content is anything that might provide insight into your show. Most often this is photos and videos, but could be a number of other things including a blog, a podcast, accompanying animated Twitter account – anything that draws attention. Most content is photos and videos, so that's what we're going to look at here, but be creative.

Photography

Photography is essential to any show. Photos will be used all over the place. In press, on social media, on theatre websites, with ticket agents, in the programme and more.

There are three specific phases of photography in most shows. These are:

- Publicity image photography
- Rehearsal shots
- Production shots

Even if you could get away without a photo shoot for your initial image, you may want to consider holding one. If you can create an image that embodies the feeling of the show, is funny or particularly striking, then it may be useful in getting feature press coverage.

I've managed this only once with a comedy about a dysfunctional father–son relationship. We managed to get a fantastic shot of the two of them, seemingly naked in the bath together. The look on their faces perfectly encapsulated the show – and it was used a ton by both feature and review coverage.

If you don't have a clear idea for a striking image and aren't having a photo for your poster image, then skip this. It's only worth it if it's going to be impactful.

Rehearsal shots are the least important of the three. They're lovely for social media, and they can accompany press stories. They also go nicely as filler for the programme, or as part of a front of house display. They are not essential pieces of content because they look the same on every show. If you have someone with profile involved, however, they are essential.

Two words of warning on rehearsal photos. Directors often don't like having them done, and particularly not in the first week of rehearsals – make sure they have okayed when a photographer is coming. Secondly, make sure all the cast are featured when you publish them. You can have your favoured images to send to press, but where you're in control of what's being used, make sure you have everyone in at least one image.

Production shots are the most important photos by miles. They are (generally) taken during your dress rehearsal. This is distinct from any press photocall where only a few scenes are shot. Here your photographer will have a whole performance to provide a large deck of photos.

These photos will accompany 95 per cent of your reviews, look great on social media, in emails, and give people a close look at the production.

The people who are most concerned about them are the lighting, set and costume designers. Hopefully, everything is finished by the dress rehearsal. Often it isn't. Consequently designers hate having the record of their show from the dress rehearsal. I don't know how to fix this, as it's the only performance you do in full without an audience there (so the photographer can wander around).

You absolutely *must* have them.

Photographers

There are many specialist theatre photographers. Inevitably they range in price, and it may be that you can find a talented friend to help you out. I wouldn't necessarily be worried about using somebody you know and trust. But I *would* be scared about ending up without any photos . . . particularly production shots. You can weigh up the cost/risk benefits.

For a long time while I was starting out I worked with a photographer who did a fringe deal where he came and took as many photos as anyone else, let me look at the whole deck, from which I chose and paid £15 each for the ones I wanted to use. For me this was the best of both worlds, a reliable professional, who cost less than £100.

These days I want more control, and have tended to do an all-inclusive deal. I pay for three shoots (image, rehearsal, production) in advance and save. But it's whatever deal you can do.

Video

More or less every production creates a trailer. A good one cuts above the noise and can make a huge difference. However, the quality varies wildly.

The main problem is budget. You're making a theatre show, but all of a sudden need to make a mini film. If you turn up with a camera and interview the actors, you'll have some content, but will it be interesting? If you spend a large section of your budget organizing a proper trailer film, will it be relevant to the show? And can you really afford it? This is an expanding industry, and people are learning fast.

Having tried a few approaches this is what I *have* learned:

- One *good* video beats three average videos
- Be clear about the purpose of the video. Probably you're trying to draw attention to the show. Think about what is eye-catching, clever and will make someone click on the link to the ticket buying page. Remember – be impactful.
- Be short. Few people will stay beyond the first three seconds. Hopefully, if it's interesting they'll hang around longer than that. But if you're trying to catch as many people as possible, get to the point fast – thirty seconds tops. I have one exception to this:
- People want to see whole songs from musicals. Your drop-off might be huge by the end, but the ones that stay are properly engaged. Just make sure the name of the show is prominent at the beginning.
- The sound is almost as important as the visual – make sure that's not forgotten.
- Make a plan, it'll save you lots of time editing. All my best trailers have been storyboarded to cover the idea of the visual, text and sound.

Talking heads

The most common theatre trailer is a simple 'talking heads'. This is the writer, director or actors talking about why people should come to see the show. These are quick and cheap to produce, and definitely better than not having a trailer. But they are common, and it's hard to stand out.

Vox pops

Vox pops are videos of audience members giving a quote to camera after a performance. Hopefully, they are still high on the energy of the performance, and will say something authentic and believable. You take short quotes and can splice them with reviews, photos or whatever else sells the show. They work because they show real people giving authentic reactions, and are quick and easy to put together.

If the show will stand up to it, I particularly like getting these in previews – sometimes even first preview (although usually only if the show has had a previous outing and I know it will be a decent standard). There's something powerful about getting a video up the morning after the first preview with reactions. You'll likely still be a way away from having reviews to talk about, and it fills a nice hole in your content schedule (as we'll see in the Schedule in Chapter 16).

'Film-style' trailer

The most impactful trailer is one that resembles what you might do for a film, to the extent you can within budget.

My most effective trailer was for a production of a romantic comedy. We took a dramatic short scene from the play where the two characters woke up in bed together after a night out. We shot it in a hotel room, and had a tight sixty-second trailer that performed exceptionally well. Crucially, it was surprising and funny. It worked as a joke, and people hung around for the punchline.

It won't work for every show. But be innovative, the key is to make it attention-grabbing and entertaining. If it's a musical it's probably about showcasing some of the songs. If it's a drama, take a look at serious film trailers. What do they do well? Film has been doing this for decades. We don't have their budget, but we can take some lessons.

Other trailers

If you don't have actors yet, consider a simple animated text and music-based trailers. Or a lyric video to accompany a song. Or . . .

I'm sure there are tons of ideas I haven't mentioned. Whatever it is, make it impactful.

Videographers

Working with a videographer is much like working with a graphic designer. Beware the ones who haven't read the play and engaged with the material. You should work closely with them, particularly on the story you're looking to tell, as you know the show and the campaign better than them. They can bring the film and video expertise.

Blogs and other content

There's no limit on what constitutes good content. Provide material that people enjoy consuming and they'll discover that your project exists, maybe think is interesting and eventually buy a ticket. It could be a blog, a podcast, a purely gif-based Twitter account, anything. But for it to be worth your time you have to be sure that people are going to engage. This requires a clear vision for who's going to consume it, and how you're going to get it to them. Speaking of which.

Distribution

Once you have created your brand and content you have to get people to see it. This is where you are competing with the big players, not just bigger theatres, but anyone trying to sell something to someone. You're going to have to be clever.

I'm breaking distribution down into:

- Email
- Organic social (all activity on social media you haven't paid for)
- Paid social (advertising on social media)
- Press (non-paid)
- Other advertising (all other paid media including outdoor, press adverts and more)

The first four are useful for you, and where you can make an impact. We'll talk about other advertising so you know what the less enticing options are.

Email

We all receive a lot of emails, from everywhere we've ever forgotten to tick the right box. Or in the case of my wife, places she actually wants to hear from. Fortunately, she is more typical than I am, which means there are people out there who want to hear about your show.

Email is great as you entirely control the content and can include all your key messaging. It is the most effective method of driving sales in theatre. After word of mouth. As long as the emails are going to the right people.

There are two groups of people that are most likely to engage with an email about your show, and won't cost you anything to contact. Your venue's email list, and you and your team's family and friends. All venues keep email addresses of people who have booked tickets in the past. These people like the venue (hopefully), know where it is and what to expect when they're there, and as such are most likely to come back. Family and friends are your family and friends!

Venue emails

Your venue email is your most effective sales driver. People who like your venue are the easiest people to attract to your show (outside of family and friends).

When you're doing the venue deal be clear on what the venue is going to offer regarding emails. You need to know how many your show will feature in, whether they will be 'solus' emails (just your show), or whether they will feature multiple shows. If the latter, where will your show feature, top, second? Also, how many people is it going to? The whole list? If not, why not? Your venue *will* want to sell tickets; however, they sometimes have different priorities than you. They may try to sell you on a 'segment' of their list, but that's only ever better for them. An example of why this might occur is if you're renting the venue, but the show following yours is produced 'in house' (by the theatre). They know the audience on their mailing list comes to 1 in 4 shows, so prioritize targeting the audience to come to their show not yours.

You want your emails to go to the widest possible segment, which is everyone.

Most likely, you will feature on all season emails, and will move towards the top as your show gets closer. The key email is the one *after* your press night. This is the number one ticket seller, as you put your reviews on it. Hopefully, this is a solus email to their whole list. At the very least you must be at the top of the newsletter.

The timing of this is key. Reviews take a while to trickle through, and it's usually worth waiting for the biggest critic who's seen the show to publish their review. My general rule (unless I get what I want immediately after press night) is to wait three to five days. But not longer as you're losing precious sales time.

PS swaps

PS swaps are small sections at the bottom of venue emails that advertise other theatres' productions. These are arranged by the venue and are a nice way of having a small presence on a new data list. Obviously, you need your venue to be involved, there's no point spending time organizing one with another theatre only to have nothing to offer in response.

Be careful that this doesn't become a large part of your strategy. It's free, so it's worth doing, but I've known whole campaigns centre around PS swaps and they simply won't have that much impact.

Friends and family

The second group of people to email is your family and friends. I find email the best way to let them know what I'm up to. As soon as you start producing the show, start asking people if you can add them to your mailing list. No one ever says no (but you do need their permission). Then you can build up a list of 100/200/300 odd people who you know are highly engaged.

The more content for any email, the better. People love seeing photos or having a trailer to watch. Use a mailing list provider like MailChimp and you can construct something that looks great. I recommend sending one every three weeks or so after the announcement of your show, and definitely an email summarizing reviews after press night.

Other email lists

It is possible to pay ticket agents to send emails to their lists on your behalf. These are worth exploring, but may be out of reach financially. If you have some *really* compelling content, or phenomenal reviews, it's more worthwhile. Otherwise, I've always struggled to see a return.

Organic social

Social media obviously provides an opportunity to promote your show, but given the competition, it can be hard to stand out. Take a look around to see who does it well, follow similar shows, follow your theatre and get a feel for what you think you can achieve.

You need to decide whether to set up new accounts in the name of the show, or whether you can manage with accounts that already exist. There are pluses and minuses to both.

I tend towards show-specific accounts, particularly these days as I work on shows that I want to have a long(er) life. If you're just planning a single two-to-three week run somewhere it might be hard to generate the followers to justify it.

Positives of a show-specific account

- You have an official place to talk about the show, release videos, information etc.
- People will immediately know how and where to get information about the show.
- You can hand them over to your company to help create content – getting your whole team involved can be really positive.

Negatives

- It can be hard to build followers for a one-off show.
- You, as the producer, don't get to take the followers with you to future shows.
- Accounts that don't manage to build sufficient followers can look a bit silly and potentially damage the brand of the show.

If you're not going to set up specific accounts, be prepared, you will have to use your personal one quite a bit. Even the most helpful theatre is only likely to want to post about your show two to three times a week, and that's not going to be enough when you get close.

Remember you need to make an impact on each channel you set up. It is better to have one channel where you make an impact than to have a mediocre performance across many.

In my experience, people respond to content, they respond to regular posts and, as with everything, they respond to humour. If you can find someone to help who has a fun social style (and it suits your show), then you're onto a winner. Accounts that mainly have 'buy tickets now!!!' messaging are boring, and people don't engage. Don't be one of them.

Paid social media

The most flexible, economical and impactful way to spend your distribution money is by promoting content on social media. They all have easy to use advertising platforms, and there's tons of literature as to how best to use them. It works because you can be extremely targeted about who sees your content. It might be groups of people who like theatre within five miles of your venue, or Jane Austen fans in a twenty-mile radius, or whatever.

This focus allows you to spend small amounts of money effectively, and not compete with big-budget shows. If it's working well, you can spend more, or if it's working badly, you can stop spending.

You can also test it in advance – promote a post to a precise group for £20 for a few days, and see what the response is. Or better, three lots of £20 to three different groups, and you can start to learn who responds best to the content. Then spend the remaining £300 (for example) on the group you know works best.

Take your time testing the creative of each post to make sure that if someone engages the content, they know that it's a theatre show and how they can learn more or buy tickets. The worst thing is to see a beautifully put together video, but learn what it's for only on the last frame, after 99 per cent of people will have switched off or scrolled past.

Worth noting that you can also promote posts from other people's pages that you don't own. You need their permission, but if your theatre pushes out something that looks great, they can give you access to promote the post, without needing to give you editing access to their page. I've done this effectively on a number of occasions.

What is *hugely* useful is if your venue can track the person who comes through social and buys a ticket. It requires them to have some technical expertise, but it is the twenty-first century. If you can track activity through to sales, you can learn and optimize your campaign, something every other industry has been able to do for a long time.

Distribution through press

If you get great content, your press rep should be able to get it distributed for free. Make sure that your rep has everything that you have *before* you distribute it through your channels, as they may be able to get an exclusive for you with some sort of theatre-specific press.

Competitions

A sneaky way to get cheap coverage is to offer free tickets to a theatre publication that they can offer out as a competition. Some may ask for you to pay, but others won't. It looks great for them to have an exclusive offer of tickets, and you get the coverage from them promoting the competition. Do this early – the slots get booked up.

Other paid distribution – advertising

It's not uncommon to see marketing campaigns that are just a list of advertising options. This is based on marketing from the wider world, where budgets are vastly different from yours.

Hopefully, you've already seen this is a small part of what marketing can be. At your budget, it's going to be the least impactful option, and is therefore the least important.

Print

Flyers and posters used to be the bedrock of marketing a show, and still feel tangible and achievable. At the Edinburgh Fringe it *is* tangible and achievable. Outside of that environment it is an expensive and non-targeted use of resources.

Some print is important. Your venue will require you to print some flyers and posters (or they'll do it for you), to put up around the venue. This is important, as attendees at the venue will often pick up a flyer of something that looks interesting. As we know they're a core audience.

Beyond that, if you are willing to spend a couple of days putting them up, posters are not a bad idea, in particular if your venue is in an area that has a local audience.

In London, be wary of anywhere with West End posters. The major marketing agencies have people who go around weekly putting up new West End shows, and you will find that your poster doesn't last long. Further, you should be looking to target people away from the West End – it's the one place where there's *no* shortage of theatre options, so you're going to get lost.

Print distribution

It is possible to pay for print distribution. Old-fashioned venues may well insist that you do. Companies offer services where they will deliver your flyers to thirty or forty places and put them in flyer racks that they have paid to be there. When you see well-organized flyer racks in pubs, theatre-front of houses, or anywhere else, that's what these are. You'll pay for a period of time in the racks, and for a certain number, and can target racks in certain types of places such as fringe theatres.

They'll also distribute posters . . . but frankly you can do that.

These companies do exactly what they advertise, and will often provide added value including listing on their website, or use of their email list. Within a large marketing budget, it's worth considering. I find that the print cost plus the distribution fee often comes to £500+, which is too much, compared to where else you could spend that money.

Leaving aside the environmental considerations, you have no idea if people are picking up the flyers, no idea what other shows you're going to be alongside and no idea how it's going to stand out. That money could make a great video that works on press, social, on emails, on websites, and will last as long as your show is on.

Adverts online or in newspapers

It is obviously possible to buy advertising space in newspapers, magazines and on websites. I wouldn't even consider it. Even West End shows struggle to have enough money to make an impact in print, as it doesn't work if you don't go big.

Online advertising is more flexible and there are more cost-effective solutions. Think carefully about whether it's going to make an impact. Are people going to really see it, notice it and click on it? Websites like WhatsOnStage and Time Out have deals that allow you take over their site for a day, which means people will definitely see it. It's worth looking at, but bear in mind that once that day is gone, so is the money.

There are companies where you can place adverts on a huge number of different websites that can be targeted based on people who've shown an interest already. When I had a £50k total marketing budget for a show, I struggled to see a return on the portion I spent on online ads. If you can track through to the sale, this has more value. Spending on Facebook (at the time) was a completely different matter.

It's also possible to buy outdoor advertising on billboards and public transport. The cost is usually measured in five-figure sums, so I'm going to leave it there.

Your company's help with selling the show

Your company are your biggest asset in terms of selling tickets. They all have friends and family, and will want them to see the show. However, they are not your marketing team.

They should participate in content and press as you need, but that's about it, in terms of what you can *expect* them to do. Beyond that, it's about providing the tools so they can easily promote the show if they want to.

Provide images and videos correctly adapted for social media, email templates and links to the show's content. Make sure the company are aware that it's up to them what they do or don't use. You may find that certain agents (particularly of the writer and director) are keen to help promote, so make sure they also have the materials.

If you decide to spend time handing out flyers, putting up posters or other labour-intensive tasks, you can't expect your company to join in, unless previously agreed, and subject to additional fees. And if it's costing you money, you can pay different people. Your company will work incredibly hard to make a great show, it's up to you to make sure there are people there to watch it!

At the Edinburgh Fringe, this still applies. However, there are greater precedents for companies getting involved with flyering. Make sure it's detailed in advance. One show I worked on, I hadn't organized it and the company didn't do it. My marketing 'strategy' was done on day one.

Remember that no one is as passionate about it as you, so don't be offended if the company aren't talking about it day and night. Some people do ten to twenty shows a year (lighting/sound designers in particular), and are unlikely to promote your show over and above any other. Similarly, the more regularly your cast are working, the more shows they have to promote and the more fatigue their nearest and dearest will have hearing about it.

Once the show is a hit, you'll find that all this changes . . .

Summary

Create a brand, create content that fits that brand and then distribute it in a thoughtful and cost-effective manner. Simple. Simpler than 'the study and management of exchange relationships' anyway.

Marketing can become a black hole for money. There are so many options, which can make focusing that money a real challenge. My key takeaway is this:

If you're not sure a spend is going to make an impact, don't do it.

It's ok not to spend the money. If you're putting everything you can into press and your sales strategy, some shows I've done have got away with just having some good images, that were shared wherever we could for free.

Paid social media posts, or posters all around town will have some effect, but unlike with press, you cannot compete with the big shows on marketing. Some of them have £100k budgets *a week* to spend. So don't try. Know who is likely to come to your show, and target them. And if you can target them for free, so much the better.

- Get photos. They're always useful. If money is tight, prioritize production shots by a professional, but get photos of everything. Phone cameras are more than good enough for social media.
- Try to get some video content. Everyone is after it. It performs better on social media and the online press love a good trailer.
- Only do one video if that's all you can afford to do well. Don't stretch one video's budget across four just because you have four ideas.

- If you try to distribute through every channel, you won't make an impact. To make an impact in every channel, you need hundreds of thousands of pounds. Let some of them go.
- Be careful about spending money in the same market as other shows, try to find ways to distribute your content where you are the unique offering.

INTERVIEW WITH STEVE TATE, FORMER HEAD OF MARKETING AT BERKELEY REPERTORY THEATRE AND ATLANTIC THEATER COMPANY, FOUNDER OF TATE THEATRICS

Steve has worked in marketing for twenty years alongside being a producer. He has worked across both London and New York, launching shows big and small, and working in pioneering early digital marketing agencies. He was also the first US marketing person involved in distributing NT Live, the National Theatre's cinema distribution programme.

Tim Johanson When you're thinking about marketing a new show where do you start?

Steve Tate I start with the artists, asking, 'What is the intention of the piece?' What is the emotional resonance that they want the audience to walk out of the theatre feeling?

Then it's my job to take the kernel of that and somehow get it into an artwork, copy, video, photos or whatever, to relay what the emotional resonance and connection an audience member is going to have, and give them a taste of it. So, they can go, 'Yes, that's something I'm interested in, I'm moved by that. I want to go see that'. The artist is the best way of getting to that.

There are professionals in this field who feel that artists are not marketers and that they don't know how to draft marketing language. But you should not be drafting 'marketing language' because people don't respond to that. People don't want to be advertised to, they don't want to be marketed to. People go to theatre because they want to be moved, because they want to be entertained, because they want to have a visceral experience in the live entertainment space.

You're not selling Coca Cola, you're not selling soap. You're not selling a consumer product that someone doesn't have a connection to. You're asking somebody to take time out of their schedule, put down some money, have a meal, get a babysitter, all of these things. It takes time and energy to do it. They want to have a good experience. It's about relaying what that experience is going to be.

But with that said the show is the thing, right? If it's a bad show or a good show, marketing moves it by degrees, but it doesn't make a show and it doesn't break a show. If you have a show that's not good and people aren't enjoying it, marketing cannot save a show.

TJ   Do you spend a lot of time working out who your audiences are?

ST   You need to be able to find who your niche audience is. For any particular show, you have at least one niche audience that you need to identify.

In this day and age of digital technology, it's pretty easy. What I tell people is do a small social ad. You can do small, targeted ads and see who clicks, because you can highly target your audiences.

So, your key metric is looking at the data and analytics of who's clicking on it. Then cross-referencing that with your website analytics data, if you have it. And that's going to give you a baseline of who is responding.

TJ   So you would get your teaser trailer, or just a basic text ad to begin with, spend £20 per segment, to three segments that you've guessed, and if one of them performs better than the others, you go, okay, I think my audience is this, and we can do another round to iterate on it, or this means we can do X, Y or Z moving forward.

ST   Right.

TJ   How important is content in terms of trying to sell something?

ST   It's key. For the performing arts, and theatre in particular, marketing is difficult when you're developing a new piece because you don't have content. You're trying to pull blood from a stone.

I hate the talking heads video, where you're just sitting down with the director and sitting down with the artist. But oftentimes that's all that you have. So you have to be creative with it.

I was doing a new show by Rajiv Joseph called *Guards At The Taj* at Atlantic Theater Company. It was a brand-new show that was getting up on its feet.

We had previously done a show by Stephen Adly Guirgis called *Between Riverside And Crazy* that won the Pulitzer. Rajiv became a writer because of Stephen. And so, I invited Stephen to come to interview Rajiv. And it was cool because Stephen had made the transition from being a playwright into the film and television world, and so these two people were talking to each other and interviewing each other in a way that no other interviewee and interviewer could have had that energy and dynamics.

That was a creative way of creating a piece of content that was a unique way to talk about the show, that is also going to bring in outside audiences, appealing to fans of Stephen's work as well.

You could go a completely other route. I worked on a slapstick comedy from an improv troupe. I got them to be in character on video, so it was not talking about the piece and it wasn't the piece itself, but it was a taste of the piece in the characters. What you do depends on the theme and the type of show, because what works with comedy may not necessarily work for drama.

TJ How do you feel about other types of content? Do they all just pale into insignificance compared to video?

ST I've done radio, audio ads, pre-rolls on podcasts, but video tends to be the easiest medium, because in the social media space, it gets the highest engagement, no matter what you're trying to sell. And then when you're trying to sell a visual visceral medium like theatre it's critical.

Also key is crafting intriguing copy that gets people to want to go on their phone, to go visit the website and find out more information.

And visual branding is important particularly if you're looking at programmatic retargeting, online banners that you're getting people's attention visually for maybe one second, two seconds. So, you want something visually intriguing.

Think about multiple impressions. People are not going to activate the first time they see something. So, if you do have a piece of content. It's getting that piece of content in multiple places.

People have to see it on social media. They have to see it in an email. They have to see it on a website. They have to see it 3, 4, 5 times before they activate on it. That's what you have to think about across the whole of your advertising and marketing – what are the different impressions and activations people can see on different platforms at different times. With the hope that the strongest piece of content is going to be the clincher. You don't ever want that piece to be the first thing, because if it is the first thing, the audience is probably not going to engage with it.

TJ If you've got a limited budget, what should the priorities be?

ST You look at all the non-monetary aspects. You get press. When your actors and designers and everyone involved on the show is active on social media, not because they have to, but because they already have a presence and because they have a passion for it, their followers are going to bring audience.

At the end of the day, it's always about word of mouth. And the best way of driving word of mouth is with content. And with social media.

TJ If you had a bit of money to spend on marketing specifically, do you have a priority list of where you would spend?

ST I would definitely put it towards trailers, towards video, towards any piece of content that you can then distribute on the free platforms.

TJ Do you have any tips for making trailers?

ST Sound is key. You want it to look and sound as professional as possible. People are going to equate the quality of your show to the quality of that video.

With that said, that doesn't mean spend an arm and a leg. There are ways of being able to do it. It's about being creative with it, get your creatives involved to at least help brainstorm.

And then have a list of where you're going to distribute it, because it's great to have a nice shiny trailer, but unless you have the right plan to distribute it, it's going to fall on deaf ears. If you want to create a one-minute-long video, how can you create a ten-, fifteen- and thirty-second version of that for the appropriate distribution channels?

You want to maximize your dollars and storyboard it and say, 'This is how we see the whole piece. And this is how we see these many pieces'. And do the many pieces stand on their own, or do they tease you to get to the larger video? What is the goal? Is it to click to the website to buy a ticket? Or is it to click to watch the larger video? Is it a series of small videos that build to a larger thing? Are you trying to build a storyline amongst all of those small videos?

There's not a right or wrong answer. What is the show that you're trying to sell? What is the theatricality of that show, and how do these videos factor into that?

TJ   You once said to me, don't be coy with content.

ST   Oh yeah, no, do not be coy with content.

You have a small amount of time and sometimes people say, 'I'm going to just give them a little bit of a taste.' No. If you have a good song, if you're working on a musical, find that hook, that Defying Gravity, that's going to drive people. Don't save it, because what's the point of saving it for the three people that come, rather than the hundreds or thousands of people that could see it, if you actually put it out there.

TJ   Who should run a campaign? You've got a limited time and money, should you hire a marketer?

ST   If you have the funds, do not hire an ad agency, hire an individual marketer, because the ad agencies, particularly the good ones, hire those individual marketers. When you work on the agency side, you do your best job when you are focused on particular shows, but on the agency's business side, they don't want you to do that because you need to be working on four or five, even six shows at once, and it's hard to give your attention. If you go the agency route, the agency will always go to the clients that have the deepest pockets.

Find somebody that maybe doesn't have a ton of marketing experience, but a passion for the show. I got involved in marketing for theatre because I have a passion for the shows, and because of the passion for the shows, I'm good at what I do. I'm not going to be a good marketer for consumer products.

TJ   My general advice is do it yourself. But I think if you have the money to get somebody, then what you just said is bang on.

And I don't even mean do it yourself. I mean, take responsibility that you are the person who has to sell tickets. What I hate is when people hire an agency or hire a marketing person, they're like, 'Oh, they weren't good, so we didn't sell any tickets'. That's not how it works. They can provide expertise and administration, and maybe ideas, but you've got to own the responsibility to sell your show.

ST   It's your piece. It's your art. No one's going to know how to do it better than you. People you hire might be able to tell you where to get the best exposure, but they're not going to be able to craft the right messaging. They can give you pointers and tips, but at the end of the day, you're the one that has the most effective information to get butts in seats.

15

Sales

The corporate world has huge departments dedicated to sales. That's because standing in front of someone and selling them something is the basis of business. From the market stall to high finance. And show business.

Being a producer is being a salesperson. We've established that. You sell to investors or funders, to the venue you want, to creatives you want for your team and then you sell to an audience.

The starting point for your sales strategy is your network. A significant percentage of people that come to your show at small scale will know someone involved in it. We all have this romantic vision that we'll put on a show and random people will come across it, think it's a good idea and buy a ticket. Well, maybe. But not many. And, definitely not at the start of the run.

Sales also includes targeting groups, ticketing agencies, ticket pricing, discounting (yuk) and complimentary tickets (big yuk).

Remember this: if something sells a ticket for your show, and is free, it's worth doing. If something sells a ticket for your show, and you know that was what sold the ticket for your show, do it again.

Using your personal network

It's nice to think that your show will automatically make an impact, that people will come because of its clever take on a contemporary issue, because it's a revival that hasn't been seen for fifty years or because it's a new musical. The reality is, the industry is huge, and standing out is seriously hard.

As we've touched on when talking about emails in the previous chapter, there *is* one group of people for whom your show already stands out, and that's your family and friends. It's nothing to do with the show, and entirely to do with you. Once you embrace this, you can provide every opportunity for them to buy a ticket without nagging them into submission.

The fewer total tickets you're trying to sell, the larger the percentage this group represents. Not relevant for a major West End show, very relevant for a week in a 100-seat studio. An early aspiration of mine was to get to a point where I could invite my family as my guests without needing them to buy a ticket. Which I know sounds ridiculous!

For a year, two years, (five years?!), you have been talking about this show. Everyone you know who's asked you what you are up to will have logged this in their minds and be potentially interested in coming to see it. You need to make sure that when it goes on sale the right people know it is happening, when it's on and have enough time to plan it into their diaries.

Use social media, an email list or a group text message, but eight to ten weeks before you begin, make sure that everyone who you think might be interested gets a clear message as to when and where it is on and how to buy tickets. This is to get it into diaries. Then a reminder a week or so before you open, and a final one with your reviews. If you do much more than that you start to nag, and your nearest and dearest won't thank you for it.

Before I was a professional, I asked a close friend whether she was coming to my show so often that she bought a ticket on the condition that I would never mention the show again. I felt bad. Sold a ticket, though . . .

Group incentives

In every group of friends or family there is someone who is good at coordinating groups of people. Identify these people and ask if they would consider organizing a group. This can be a group of people you know, or even better, a group of people you don't. It might be an office outing, a friend bringing their family or something else.

The trick to make this seem like an offer from you, rather than a nagging ask, is to offer a group discount. 'If you could pull together ten people, I can knock 15 per cent off.' Unless your show is selling out, there is no downside to this. It is unlikely that all the people in the eventual group would have come independently, and your seats are available. They come, they enjoy it and they tell other people to come. Ideal.

Social media sales

It is possible to approach people specifically on social media who have shown an interest in a relevant topic. This is delicate and something I've never done, but I watched Kevin (whom I've interviewed in the appendix) doing it effectively. There was a show on in the West End that was selling out, called *Chimerica*. He was producing his show *Yellow Face* at the time, and figured that people interested in one might be interested in the other. So he searched for terms on Twitter and wrote a polite individual message to say that if they'd enjoyed *Chimerica*, then they should check out *Yellow Face*.

I don't know how well it did, but he got a number of replies saying that people absolutely would check it out, and I'm sure he sold tickets off the back of it.

This could go badly if you got the tone wrong, or made the wrong association between two shows. But handle it carefully and maybe it'd be right for you.

Ticketing agencies

I didn't know anything about ticketing agencies until I did my first big show. I'd definitely have used them before if I'd known how they worked.

Ticketing agencies are organizations that sell tickets on your behalf to their mailing lists of previous bookers. Ticketmaster, See Tickets, Encore – you will have used them to book tickets for gigs, sports or theatre. Theatre-specific agencies include TKTS and TodayTix.

Ticket agents have access to people that you don't. They have huge mailing lists, and data about who books for what and where. They sell your tickets, and take a cut on the inside of the ticket (usually). So your £20 ticket, which you'd usually get £20 off, you now get £16, because they're taking £4. If you wouldn't have sold the ticket anyway, then you haven't lost anything. Crucially, there is no upfront cost. As someone put it to me, if you could guarantee £16 of sales for every £4 of marketing spent, would you do it? Of course, you would.

Before you get too excited you need to speak to your venue. It requires some technical knowledge to set up, and if they don't have the ticketing software that integrates with the agency, an ongoing box office labour cost. Ideally, they'll already be set up with certain agencies.

In using them, the negotiations are around the size of commission, in return for marketing activity. They will say, 'Give us 25 per cent of the ticket price, and we will send a solus email to 50k people'. Up to you to work out if that's a good deal. It probably is . . .

As with marketing, make it impactful. If one agency would be interested in exclusivity, and as a result will give you three mailouts, social coverage and one of three slots in the Evening Standard advert they're taking out, that's better than limited support across three agencies.

A few notes:

- It takes time to set up. If you're going to do it, start immediately, don't punt it down the road.
- Ticket agencies have historically been considered 'not classy'. They represent shows that can't make it by themselves, and need to use them. You haven't seen Harry Potter or the National Theatre using

them. For you this should not be important, selling a ticket is hard enough. And the rise and rise of TodayTix is changing opinions anyway.

- Invite the agency to send their agents to previews. They won't pay, but if they love your show, then maybe they'll push your show to undecided punters.
- If you start selling out, *pull your tickets from the agency*! At that point they're taking an unnecessary cut. If it's a sellout, people will come to the venue website to buy their ticket and you can have 100 per cent of the ticket price.

At the time of writing, agencies work in two ways. One (the old school) is the box office, which gives an exclusive allocation of tickets to each agency and blocks them out on the core box office. The agency then sells them, and gives back unsold tickets on the day of the performance. This requires your box office to manually manage this return of tickets. It's a lot of work and, frankly, unrealistic for most small venues. There's then a worst-case scenario of tickets held by the agency unsold, but people not being able to buy a ticket elsewhere, because it looks like it's sold out.

Far better is the agency integrating with your venue's box office directly. This allows them to sell any ticket in the house (better for them) without tickets looking unavailable on the venue website (better for you). In time this will be the way the whole industry works – for now they both exist.

Pricing

The bigger your venue, the more complicated ticket pricing becomes. In smaller venues there are fewer options.

Many venues have a fixed ticket price that they're not willing to negotiate. That's usually good enough at the small scale. If they have flexibility, have a think about what you would be willing to pay for something similar, or what similar shows are charging. If in doubt, split the difference between the cheapest and most expensive tickets at your venue.

You're better off having a slightly high price rather than slightly low. It's always possible to offer discounts, but it's not really possible to raise the price. If you have a hit, you'll find your ticket price doesn't look expensive after all.

Discounting

Discounting is tricky. If you're struggling to sell tickets, particularly in advance, you'll receive advice saying 'well why don't you just offer a discount?' In many businesses this is an effective way of increasing the number of products sold.

Your core audience are people connected to the production. If they haven't booked a ticket, it's probably not because of the price. I've seen little evidence of discounting being effective until shows get big. For a discount to hit home, you need a *lot* of people who've heard of the show but are looking for a bargain. Your problem will be that not enough people have heard of the show.

People will, however much they love you, take you up on the discount. So people who were coming anyway are just getting to pay less.

Discounting also impacts the perceived success of the show. Successful shows don't discount. At some point you may have to swallow your pride and try to coax people in any way you can, but avoid doing this in advance of the run. It gives a negative message, just when you need positivity.

There are a few exceptions that can help:

- Previews should be cheaper. This isn't a discount as it's the ticket price from the start. It allows you to drive your audience into early performances and maximize word of mouth.
- Early-bird offers work. But they must be put out there at the announcement of the show. The narrative is 'even before we've tried to sell tickets, we'll give you a discount for booking early'. There must be a closing date, it must be only for previews or the first ten or so performances and you must stick to it. Once it's gone, it's gone.
- Group discounts are great. Every show does it.
- Targeted 'flash' sales are ok (short period sales, usually 24 hours). Particularly if done by a ticket agent with a mailing list of people that you can't get to. Don't mention it on your channels and by the time it's done its work, it will have disappeared.

Make sure just after your reviews come out that there are no discounts available. This will allow all your lovely sales on the back of reviews to be full price.

None of this is gospel. Ultimately you have to do whatever to get people in. If you do feel you have to cut prices in order to get anyone to come – try it, and if it fails, pull the offer and try something else. And if it does wonders, please let me know!

Complimentary tickets

Complimentary tickets (comps) are something that every producer battles with. There are two types: company comps, and papering comps. Company comps are people you and your company would like to see the show. Papering is when your show is so empty that you're willing to give tickets away to get an audience.

Company comps

Ridiculously, given everything that's come before, the only thing I've fallen out with people about on shows is comps. Seriously.

Nobody in your company will be doing your show purely for the money. Nobody. So what are they doing it for? To be seen, or to have their work seen. And if you make a great show, this will only increase.

It is vital to have a comps policy set out in advance. What that policy is, is up to you. If you don't have one, you will have so many comp requests, you won't know what to do with them. It can genuinely run to the hundreds. And if you start granting them early on, you can be *sure* that they will increase. Everyone loves a free ticket, not everyone understands the consequences this has on a producer.

My policy is pretty harsh. I set up a discounted company rate for tickets (15 per cent to 25 per cent off) that they can give to anyone they want, I give everyone as many comps as I can on press night (usually a pair), and after that, zero. It's the only policy I've ever managed to stick to.

Other policies I've tried is a comps for industry only (I warn you there's a lot), or four to six per company member throughout the run. Whichever it is, be prepared to stick to it. And to follow it yourself.

The reason you're not destroying the careers of your artists is that industry pays for tickets. All the time. Agents always pay. So do casting directors. They'll appreciate the company discount, but they absolutely should pay. If your director persuades Michael Grandage or Marianne Elliot to come and see their work, *they should pay*. Established people in the industry can afford it. They'll accept a comp out of politeness, but should understand how hard it is to finance small theatre productions.

I am aware that I'm harsh on this. If you have unrepresented actors in the show, and they have persuaded an agent to come, they're going to hate not being able to offer a comp. It's really hard. Be clear upfront one way or another and you'll be fine.

A quick side-note: it is essential that *only* you are able to book comps with box office. No one should be able to just put them through without asking you. It sets a horrible precedent and is unfair on the people who wouldn't have the gall to do it. Your venue should police this for you. And yes, this is, unfortunately, where my falling out occurred.

Papering

Papering is the practice of giving tickets away through organizations with private mailing lists, in order to get people into your show. The mailing list is private, and is not supposed to have anyone from the industry on it. Members of the list have strict instructions about being discreet and staying until the end. You get an audience, and no one is any the wiser.

There is nothing as bad as an empty audience. It demoralizes the actors, and you never get good word of mouth when the audience is sparse. As such, once you've tried everything else, you might need to paper your show.

I know this directly contradicts the previous section about not giving comps. Sadly, the people your company would like to offer comps to, might all buy a ticket. The people on these waiting lists are just waiting for freebies.

For a small show you should be able to get six to eight people per show if you offer in enough time. Hopefully that'll make the difference between twelve people in the audience and twenty. Twenty people in most studios is just fine! Unfortunately, it's not a given that you'll even be able to paper a show. Sometimes you just can't find the people to give them away to . . .

Don't tell your company. They may find out, but don't advertise it. It is demoralizing and if you've spent your time being firm about comps on one hand, and on the other, are offering free ones to random people it can be hard to explain. It *is* totally justified, but they may not see it that way. Hopefully, you can avoid papering. It is seriously painful.

Sales reports

Your box office will automatically send you sales reports, from the day you go on sale. I like these to come daily, but weekly is fine for the first few months. Once you get within six weeks, you'll definitely want them daily, in order to track whether your marketing activity has any effect. I then plot a basic graph of cumulative sales against date to keep an eye on how we're going.

Audience data

One might presume, given all of this effort to sell a show, that you might be able to know something about the people who've come to see it. Unfortunately, it is regarded across the industry that audience data is owned by the venue. It's a big fight. Producers, rightly, believe they produced the show, so it should be their data. Venues think that the audience has come to their venue, so it should be theirs. Probably it should be both, but data legislation prevents that.

An (expensive) way around this is to set yourself up as a ticket agent, and sell tickets through a show website. This relies on venue cooperation and a partnership with a ticket agent for your website, and is probably out of reach for you.

This is the single biggest thing keeping theatre sales and marketing in the Dark Ages. Here's hoping that by the time you read this, we have a better solution.

Summary

It amazes me that we don't talk more about sales in theatre. It wasn't until I'd worked on a six-figure show that it even came up, and then it was only ticketing agencies. Yet, it's the perfect way to sell a ticket if you can. It's free. You can do as much of it as you have time and energy for. And it's in your control. You're not reliant on a journalist, or your social media taking off. It's just your being a salesperson. Lean in to it.

- Embrace the fact that your network is your primary audience. Make their life as easy as possible to buy a ticket.
- Talk to your venue about ticketing agencies. They're a great resource.
- Avoid discounting before you open. It's not what will make people buy a ticket at that stage.
- Come up with a comp policy early.
- Don't be afraid to paper the show if you have to.

It would be possible to do a show purely on the back of a publicity image and sales strategy. I don't recommend it. But it is *that* important.

INTERVIEW WITH TICKET AGENT MARC PEACHEY, SENIOR DIRECTOR OF PARTNERSHIPS AND TICKETING AT TODAYTIX GROUP

Marc is a senior member of TodayTix Group's large team based in London, having been one of the first employees when TodayTix launched in the UK. He has worked in ticketing for many years, from theatre box office to his position today.

Tim Johanson   How do you find working with smaller theatres as a ticket agent?

Marc Peachey   The issue that you come up against with smaller venues is the resource on the venue side by way of box office team. The box office manager might have three or four other roles in the venue. So they can't work with many ticket agents, they might only be able to work with one.

TJ   Why is that?

MP   It's to do with the API integration. If, for instance, you're on Spektrix's box office system, most agents are integrated with Spektrix, which means the process is streamlined.

Where you don't have that, you are relying on the manual day-to-day management of an allocation of tickets. So with a lot of the smaller venues, they will either not work with the agents because they don't understand the landscape or they don't have the means of doing it.

TJ   If there's a venue which doesn't have a ticketing system that you integrate with, it needs a box office person who's willing to take on the workload?

MP   Yeah, without doubt.

TJ   What can producers do to help you do the most for them?

MP   A lot of people only approach us last minute. 'We've got the show. It starts in two weeks. Can you help?' By the time we have everything we need it'll be too late, I might need seventy artwork assets to get that show live.

TJ   That many?

MP   It can be, depending on whether we're sending it out across our entire network. Typically it should be between fifteen and twenty. But if you're doing stuff across our affiliate network, it can be as high as that. Everyone's got different specifications for their email, website etc.

So late approaches don't leave us enough time to a) get on sale and b) have time to actively sell the production. We're just not going to have enough time to make a meaningful difference to sales. We need to be involved more or less from the outset.

TJ   Once you are up and running, is there anything that producers can do to help you do the best for their show?

MP   Be receptive to ideas about how we can push the show to other audiences outside of the app. Not being too precious about it, which is difficult when you're close to a show and it's hard to think of it as a product.

With smaller shows we will do as much as we can. It depends whether or not it fits into the life cycle of our schedules, as to what size opportunity we can give.

There's a little bit of naivety across venues and producers about what our role is. There's a bit of received wisdom that we take away from the industry rather than add to it. Our job is to dispel that and promote a collaborative relationship.

TJ   Tell me about the £15 ticket offer?

MP   £15 has become a TodayTix calling card. We did a successful offer kind of at that price point Off-West End recently.

On things like that we know people will respond quickly. Volume-wise that might sell 300 tickets, which for us wouldn't be huge, but potentially massive for someone else.

We did an Off-West End promo and the top-selling show there sold 1,100 tickets, which again we think isn't a huge figure, but for the size of the venue you're selling into and the duration of run it could be quite meaningful.

TJ   What are the deals that work best for both sides?

MP   It depends what you need. Off-West End pricing is restrained, so you don't have anywhere near as far to go in terms of making a compelling offer to a consumer. If you've got an offer on a £85 West End ticket going at £35, you can boast about a tremendous saving. Small venues can't do that.

So think about what you need from it. Whether you're interested in driving volume, you've got a lot of performances to shift in a short space of time, or whether it's actually, we just need to do something across mid-week performances. In either case we can tailor something to the needs of the individual show and price points that we know works with our audience.

16

Campaign schedule

The final piece in the ticket-selling puzzle is to put your press, marketing and sales activity together in a schedule. In order to maximize visibility, you want concentrated bursts of activity. This allows potential audience members to experience your activity from multiple sources at a similar time, and make a bigger impact. I think a marketing professional would call it having a 'joined-up strategy'!

The moments for this activity are quite natural – your show announcement, cast announcement, first rehearsal, first preview and press night. Focus your resources around these areas and people will watch the buildup of the show and be desperate to see it by the time it opens. Hopefully. You'll have periods of quiet where you're not doing very much, particularly pre-rehearsals, but that's ok. It's expensive to be 'noisy' for more than a few weeks, and spreading your resources thinly will reduce your impact.

There is no hard and fast rule. This schedule is meant to illustrate how one particular campaign might go. Yours could be completely different. If you've thought about who you're trying to get to and how you're going to get to them, you'll be fine.

After venue confirmation

Once you've green-lit the show, you need to start thinking about how you're going to sell it. At this stage it's not about trying to sell tickets (you're not yet on sale) but about preparation for your show announcement and beyond.

Press

- Start talking to press reps. This is a two-way thing. You're trying to work out whether they'll do a good job, and they're trying to work out whether you'll be a good client to work with.

Marketing

- If you haven't got them already, start working on your image and marketing copy.
- Could you come up with a cheap trailer to accompany your show announcement? Graphic and text-based? A quick interview with the writer and director? Or are you going to hold back your cash until you have cast and can do one quality trailer?

Sales

- Start thinking about sponsorship or partnership opportunities. Who might be interested in supporting the show? If not supporting with cash, then who is it who might send an email with the show's details to their email lists? Even a small ask like that can take months to get through, so start early.
- Set up ticketing agencies. Find out who's already set up on the box office. Would an agency like a twenty-four-hour exclusive on sale before you release tickets more widely? (Exclusive to them *plus* the theatre box office, just no other agencies.) What are they going to give you in terms of marketing support?
- Set up a group rate for agencies and for you.

Show announcement

The first opportunity to talk publicly is your show announcement, when you tell the world it's happening, and put tickets on sale. This is the starting gun for the campaign.

Press

- Your announcement press release goes now – your rep can begin talking to journalists.

Marketing

- Begin your social media accounts.
- Release your poster image online.
- Begin to put up your posters (if they're ready).
- Send venue email and one to your private email list (that you've been compiling).

Sales

- The show goes on sale. Some major shows can have separate announcements and on-sale dates, but it's unlikely you'll generate coverage twice, so do them at the same time.
- Early-bird ticket offer up and running.
- Any ticket agencies set up and ready to help with the launch.

Cast announcement

You might release the cast with the show announcement. It's not a bad idea to do it separately, if both will make an impact. If you feel either is non-impactful, do them together. One impact is better than two non-impacts.

Press

- Depending on whom you've cast, your rep may want to send another press release announcing casting.

Marketing

- Release photos of the cast members, or even better, a trailer involving the cast.
- You should now be on all venue emails going out, underneath the current shows.

Sales

- Send ticket agencies updated marketing materials, and send a reminder to anyone helping you to arrange a group.

Start of rehearsals

This is where the excitement ramps up. You have the entire team together for the first day of rehearsals, and a great opportunity to get social content in particular.

Press

- Any feature interviews will happen during rehearsals, and be released in the two weeks leading up to the run. If you've held your trailer until now, can your rep get a publication to post it as an exclusive?

Marketing

- Great social opportunity. Short video clips from the meet and greet. Photos of the read-through or people seeing the model box for the first time. Social media users in the company are bound to send something today about their first day.
- Your competitions should be running around now.
- You should be very prominent on any venue emails, top or second from top, and use first-day content to distribute through your private email list.
- Get promoting your trailer through social media.

Sales

- Any early-bird discounts should be long gone. Drive people to previews through the cheaper ticket price.

Previews

Once you get to your first preview, you'll be through tech, dress and will be knackered. It's the busiest, most exhilarating time, but it's important not to forget about selling tickets. It's easy to get lost solving technical problems or creative issues, but this is a time of key momentum.

It's your final opportunity to draw attention to the show before reviews. Remember, you want your reviews to be the second or third hit, the push over the line to booking a ticket, not the first. So keep grafting.

Press

- This is all about press night now. You or your rep should be following up with the critics, trying to get them to book in.

Marketing

- You should have production photos from the dress rehearsal. Can your rep place them for an exclusive with a theatre website? If you have lots of great shots, hold a few back, and you can release 'new' or 'unseen' shots at a quiet moment later. Once they are released, make sure everyone has them – particularly ticket agencies.
- Release any vox pops you've filmed – a perfect way to draw attention. Did you manage to find someone well known to come along? Ideal.

Sales

- If you've got fewer than twenty tickets available for a performance, that's great messaging. Fewer than ten . . . maybe it's time to hold them off sale and shout about being sold out? Up to you – nothing is more attractive than something you can't get.

Press night

A terrifying night . . . and a great chance to create a buzz.

Press

- Crucial night – make sure you've got your press tickets and programmes sorted, sit back and cross your fingers they like it.

Marketing

- This is all social. People arriving, pictures of press night gifts, excited cast members backstage – there are tons of photo/video opportunities. Standing ovation at the end? Hope you had your phone ready to capture it.
- Take photos of anyone prominent who's come to watch – even if it's just the team. They'll be useful ideally for press, but also for social.

Sales

- Hold fire. We're waiting for reviews, but make sure your agencies are ready to push the tickets when the reviews have come. What do they need from you to be most effective?

After press night

At this stage, if you've done your job right, loads of people know your show is happening, are interested and need that final push over the line.

Press

- Presuming not all press came on press night, your rep is going to keep pushing critics to come in throughout the run. Even if The Times came only on the last night, it could provide a review that gives the show another life.

Marketing

- Your venue email goes. The most important moment of the run. Make sure it looks great.
- I have a 'reviews image' made using a production shot with the best review quotes and stars on. I can distribute it to the company, put it on social media and send it to my personal email list.
- Keeping social media up through a short run isn't too hard. By the time you've used the reviews, and excited reaction from audiences who've come to watch, it'll be time for 'two weeks to go' messaging. If you happen to have a longer run, you need to think about what could be new to talk about.

Sales

- Start to look at ticket offers if you need to. If you're giving a ticket offer through an agent, they need to give marketing support to promote it. Offers through ticket agents are much less damaging to the 'brand' of the show than offers on social media. Particularly through the official channels or the cast.

Summary

The biggest reason to work out a schedule in advance is to avoid missing opportunities. The first big show I produced was littered with missed opportunities. Would the show have been a hit if I'd taken all the sales opportunities I had? Who knows? But I'm still bothered by the idea that it might have been.

There's no right schedule out there. I hope this one is helpful as an example.

- Think about your campaign moments for activity before you start and target at them.
- Your venue email with your reviews is the most important one to get right.
- Be flexible and take opportunities if they arise. Your campaign plan is a great starting point, but not set in stone.

Part III – Conclusion

Right now I imagine you're feeling pretty overwhelmed. There's a lot to do and understand. And you're doing all of this whilst you're probably trying to general-manage the show as well.

- You can't do it all. Don't panic if you only manage half of what's here. I've never managed to do all of this.
- Make sure the general management doesn't derail the selling of the show. You will bring in every ticket through blood, sweat and tears, and if you're distracted by practical stuff, you won't be focused on the one thing that no one else is doing. I produced one show that had a disastrous final two weeks of rehearsals that took all of my time. You could see on the sales curve the specific day I stopped selling to help save the creative.
- If you can find people to help who are as motivated as you, then *do*. Just be careful of agencies who will suggest strategies that work on the West End, but don't understand the graft on a smaller scale.
- Find a press rep. If you possibly can. Their contacts are so hard to replicate.

PART IV

Edinburgh Fringe Festival and how to maximize a hit

17

Edinburgh Fringe

The starting point for many theatre makers is the Edinburgh Fringe. It was where I fell in love with theatre, and I think it's the most wonderful place. However, it's governed by its own rules. Most of what I've written previously applies in theory, but one way or another Edinburgh sits at the extremes.

Why it's great

- Edinburgh is the single best place in the *world* for new acts to get seen. By critics, by venues, by promoters, by producers. Whatever you're after, they are in Edinburgh in August.
- The networking is incredible. Both British and international. I'd guess that more than 75 per cent of the British theatre industry have taken a show at some point. The next movers and shakers in the industry will have a show at Edinburgh. The best thing about taking a show to Edinburgh is being a part of the festival.
- It's inexpensive. Bear with me. It is inexpensive, relative to London certainly, to put on a show in Edinburgh in terms of total costs and for that show to have significant impact. There's essentially zero production budget (no set, limited lighting), and the venue typically take a cut of ticket income, not a full rental. Shows are smaller and audiences, critics and the industry expect less. That's not to say it's not costly (see next section . . .).
- Fun. Boy, can it be fun. Not always. Not if your show doesn't do well. But it can be the greatest place in the world.

Why it's difficult

- Everyone knows it's a great place to be seen. So everyone goes to be seen. The competition is huge. For everything. Which means:

- There is a serious risk of no one coming. Shows regularly play to two or three people. If you're not prepared for the realities of Edinburgh, then you'll get a horrible shock. Just because there's a huge audience in the city does not mean there's a huge audience for your show.
- Sales relate to the time you put in. Which means there's no down time. Shows sell so many of their tickets through flyering that you need to be out there. It makes for long days.
- No days off. Traditionally shows take one day off in the month. It's super-tiring.
- It's personally expensive. When you budget at 10 per cent sales capacity, as you should, it won't add up. Which means that one way or another, you're going to have to subsidize it. Additionally, you're away from home, so you can't do your day job. Then there's watching shows, eating out every day, etc. etc. If you have a hit, and have some box office at the end, *the best* you can hope for is to break even. It's such a great thing to do, but you have to be financially prepared. This has a huge impact on access.
- To add insult to injury, there's no government subsidy available for Edinburgh. From Arts Council England at least. (It's not *quite* that simple, but broadly speaking.)

Advice

If you are going to go, and are confident about making the money work:

- Know why you are doing it. Is it for promoters to help tour the show? Critics to boost your profile? To network? For fun? Whatever it is, be clear and focus on it. It will help with the inevitable roller coaster that is Edinburgh.
- Prioritize a press rep. An experienced Edinburgh specialist ideally. It's almost impossible to stand out without one.
- Budget at 10 per cent capacity. Seriously. Anything more and you're not taking into account the worst-case scenario. (10 per cent might not be the worst-case scenario . . . .)
- Don't overdo design – no one else is. You can probably do without much of a design at all. Your director might disagree. Your biggest cost is accommodation. If they insist, find a lighting/sound designer based in Edinburgh. Or already being taken up there by another (bigger) show.
- Do everything you can to get into the better venues. I hate this advice. I wish all venues were equal in Edinburgh, it feels like that's how it should work. But it's not the case. There's a scale of

reputations. They do change. Ask around for advice, or ideally, go up the previous year and see for yourself.

- Make sure your show is ready for *show one* in Edinburgh. Find somewhere to put the show on before you get there for previews. You'll then be able to invite critics on day one, giving you a vital boost.

- See each other's shows. It may seem counter-intuitive, but if you can get to the other shows in your venue (you'll be allowed in for free with your venue pass), it will help start the word of mouth. It's super-hard to get audiences for your first few shows, so ten people per show using their venue passes to come in is a great boost, particularly if you have a critic in.

- Hire a street team of flyerers (if you can). It can be only one or two people. Make sure to involve them as a key member of the team, so they can become passionate about the show. It's impossible to track what a flyerer is actually doing, so you have to trust them and someone who loves the show is easier to trust. Having some form of street team will give you security that if you have to be in the venue sorting the show, someone is trying to sell tickets.

Summary

Edinburgh is an amazing place to put on work and it can be the fastest way to industry recognition, which is why it is so popular. But it's also the Wild West, and can be a brutal place if it's not going well.

- Get completely on top of the finances. Budget at 10 per cent for your first show.
- Try to employ a press rep and a street team if you can.
- If you go, be clear about the top outcome you're after, and focus your energies on achieving that.

INTERVIEW WITH PRODUCER FRANCESCA MOODY, FOUNDER OF FRANCESCA MOODY PRODUCTIONS

Francesca is an experienced producer, working on new work from the small scale to the West End. The original producer of *Fleabag*, Francesca has had particular success working in Edinburgh and has become one of the most respected Fringe producers.

Tim Johanson   Why put on shows in Edinburgh?

Francesca Moody   It's a free marketplace. We produce new work there and we use it as a launch pad.

    If you can get work to the Fringe, it is quite a level playing field. The Artistic Director of the National Theatre or lead critic at The Guardian can come and see your show. And if you were producing your show elsewhere you might not have that same opportunity. Weirdly, despite the market of Edinburgh being incredibly saturated, there's that potential.

    The other reason is it is a great base to build from. You've got a captive audience in Edinburgh, with a festival mindset – audiences go to Edinburgh to see shows. So if you get it right, you can really build a fizz around a show, which can help propel the next phase of production. It's an epic month-long showcase.

TJ   What's the best-case scenario for a run in Edinburgh?

FM   Most of the time Edinburgh isn't about making money. In the dream version, you sell out your show, obviously, because the more money you take, the less money you lose in Edinburgh, and that's good.

    But for me, success is all the other stuff. Making partnerships and relationships with future co-producers, future venues, a tour, a commercial transfer or a London run for a show. The best version of Edinburgh is whatever you want to get out of Edinburgh. Which sounds like a bit of a cop-out answer, but Edinburgh can be lots of different things.

TJ   So it might be reviews, or it might be touring venues . . .

FM   Or it might be a New York transfer, or it might just be about profiling your work and your company. If you're an artist producing, it might be about putting yourself on the map a bit.

    Eddie Izzard was at an event I went to and we had a discussion about the Fringe for her. She did years before people knew who she was. So for artists who are self-producing it can also just be about putting yourself in people's eyeline.

It's important to think about what you want to get out of it. It is expensive, it is sort of relentless and it is incredibly demoralizing at times. It's all the good things that I said, but there are 3,000 other shows there.

TJ And is the worst-case scenario none of the above?

FM I think the worst-case scenario is not achieving any of that, at all.

TJ Presumably then you've lost money by design, and then extra on top.

FM Yeah. The worst-case scenario is losing your own money, which a lot of people do. I thoroughly encourage people to try not to spend their own money or risk their own money. Try and raise all the money that they need to put on the show rather than budget on box office.

As a side note, if Edinburgh is not about making money and if you are new or it's your first or your second time, think about venue capacity, not in the context of how much money you can make, but in the context of trying to create an energy around your show.

The game that you play in Edinburgh is to try and sell out your show. Because as soon as you start selling out, it's one of the best marketing tools for your show. Not just getting on the sold-out board, but the domino effect on audiences, and on the industry as well. As soon as your show sells out, the industry is much more likely to sit up and notice. The press as well. If you can afford to, find a fifty-, sixty-seat venue. *Fleabag* was in a sixty-seat venue.

TJ How important are the different venues?

FM Anybody who's thinking about taking work to the Fringe, in an ideal world, would go first and experience it for yourself.

More than the physical spaces themselves, it's worth understanding the external perceptions of those venues, and what kind of work they tend to programme. It's also worth knowing location-wise what the vibe is, because some venues have a real fizz and energy to them. And some don't.

It's about positioning your show for the industry in particular. It might not matter if you are producing a show that is pure audience entertainment and didn't really matter what the industry thought. But if you're producing a new play that you want to have a life, find somewhere classy to present it, so that the industry is going, 'Oh, I always go there because the work there's good, interesting and challenging'.

TJ Do you find that tech and running time limitations affect the ongoing life?

FM   No, I don't, because Edinburgh is the start of something, most of
the time. If you want a future life, your show is contingent on the
industry – the industry knows what Edinburgh is.

Where people fall down is if you try to create the all-bells-and-
whistles version of your show and you can't because it's Edinburgh.

TJ   How do you go about selling a ticket in Edinburgh?

Franceca Moody   You have to have a good image for your show. Don't
overcomplicate it. If you are struggling to come up with an image in
the short amount of time you have for the registration deadline, the
only place that is ever committed to is the brochure. You can change
it on the internet, and that's where everybody goes these days.

So simple things, good copy, great image. Plunder the depths of
everybody's previous successes to add credibility. Who in your team
has been involved in a show that has had four stars or a Fringe First,
or whatever.

There are some things that you have to think about early if you
want to do them. Print marketing still plays a massive role in a way
that we are moving away from everywhere else in the country. But
flyers still matter. Posters still matter. People look for them. So think
about those early on.

My big thing is getting a good press rep because press is really
helpful in Edinburgh. At the least you want to try and get your rep to
get you into some of the top ten recommendations. That's the best bit
of marketing ever, pre-Fringe.

Whatever you are comfortable with, but as early as possible, get
the press to see your shows. The earlier you are comfortable with
having press, the easier it will be to get critics in.

And then when you're there, word of mouth is crazy important.
One of the first things you should do is make friends with the box
office and front house staff. They are people that everyone asks,
'what should I go and see?' So make friends with them. They really
will sell your show.

Sell out your show, obviously! With a small capacity.

Twitter plays a big part as well – it's everything in terms of
recommendations, what people think.

Flyering is still a big thing. We have our own small street team,
whom we try to make feel part of our team. We bring them to the
shows, take them for drinks etc. In Edinburgh think about the
quantity of posters and then the quality of conversation in the selling
of your show.

And then there are random things that you can do to help create
a bit of a brand for your show in Edinburgh. People love to give out
badges or stickers . . .

And also lean on your peers. There's a lot of cross-pollination,
working out who your peers are and whether you can do flyer swaps,

whether you can put your flyers on their seat in their venue, all of that stuff. Those are easy, quick wins.

Peer-to-peer advocacy is important 10 per cent, 15 per cent, 20 per cent of your audience are people who are doing shows.

Also there used to be a stat years ago that 70 per cent of your audience is Scottish or something like that. So don't forget that the best use of papering tickets is going into hairdressers and taxi companies, and giving them some free tickets. They're always recommending and talking to people. People who actually live and work in Edinburgh and who have customer-facing jobs. They'll take a free ticket and they will definitely talk about your show if they like it.

TJ   Final question. What are the biggest mistakes you see people making?

FM   Putting their shows in venues that are too big. Capacity-wise.

And not thinking about their audience. Who is this for? Which is basic 101, but artists in particular sometimes forget to think about it when they just want to make something. Niche subjects that don't have a hook are really hard to sell in Edinburgh.

18

Maximizing the impact on your career

In Chapter 1, I presumed that you were here to *start or progress a career in the arts*. It's (clearly) a lot of work to put on a show. But how can all that work help with the reason for setting out in the first place?

This chapter is going to look at what happens if and when you make something good.

What to do if you have a hit?

If you get good reviews and good word of mouth, you may start to sell a lot of tickets. In that case, you have a hit. People are enjoying the show and telling their friends to come see it. Fantastic.

What now?

- Maximize the hit.
- Focus on the future of the show.
- Increase your network.

Firstly, maximize the hit. Make sure every ticket possible is available to be sold. This means releasing your producer holds every day, ensuring the venue are releasing their holds in time and making sure ticket agencies aren't sitting on allocations of tickets.

Push your press rep for the remaining critics to come. At this stage it's about using reviews for the future of the show as much as selling tickets. Remember, critics follow one another to hit shows, so keep pushing.

For the future of the show you need to get people in who can help give it another life. There may be an obvious place to transfer your show, or maybe the show would work on tour. Alternatively, if it's gone really well it may be the show has a much greater scale and a larger producer might take it on.

If it's new, there may be exciting opportunities in other mediums, on screen or otherwise.

Prepare a short summary of the show, the reviews and a few pictures. Work out whom you need to write to and write to them. If you've got a hit, it'll all come more easily.

Most people won't get around to seeing it, therefore it's essential you get a video recording of the show. A one-camera shoot may be the best you can manage. If you can do more, great. If the show's good, lots of people will end up watching the video. Like when shooting a trailer, the sound is as important as the video itself.

When you have a show on, it's the perfect time to grow your network. You have something people will have heard about, and have an easy conversation starter. Write to everyone you think could help with your career inviting them to the show. Follow up with anyone who comes after the show's done. If you can get a coffee with someone, then that's a win.

Finally, having a hit is why we produce. So enjoy it!

Inviting industry to your show

How are you going to get industry people to come?

Whether you've met them before or not, the approach is the same.

- Send them an email with the details at least three weeks before you open. Early enough for their diaries to have some space. If you can get someone to introduce you, it helps massively.
- Follow up with a summary of the best reviews shortly after you open.
- If you've heard nothing, send an email after the end of the run summarizing the whole thing.

That's it. If you hassle people beyond that, they still won't come, and you do yourself damage in the long run. For context I receive three to four of these approaches a week, and probably see the show one time in fifty. It doesn't mean you haven't got a good show – people are busy.

The key things that attract me from the first email are:

- It is addressed to me, with a personal message. If it's a generic mailout I don't even read it. Silly thing, an ego, isn't it!
- All the information is present.
- That it is written like it's an invitation to an industry member. I know where Theatre503 is. Don't spend a paragraph explaining it and its history.
- It is a polite invitation that acknowledges it's unlikely, but on the off chance 'I wanted to let you know'.

These may all seem obvious, or petty. But if you want someone to take you seriously, flatter their ego a little, be friendly and polite.

The second email:

- Is a concise follow-up.
- Has your best reviews or perhaps particular audience feedback. Maybe it includes your lovely production shot reviews image.

Really, here I'm only attracted by whether the show is good. And, realistically, that means the reviews. Other different industry types will feel differently (casting directors care far more about an actor's performance, for example).

You will get very few replies. It'd be amazing if that wasn't the case, but it is. Everyone is busy. And no one likes sending the email that's possibly a lie, 'I'm too busy', or the truth, 'I have other things that I'd rather be doing'. Don't take it personally.

Start from an expectation of zero replies, react to any interest as a positive and no response as the expected outcome. That way you can only be pleased.

One of the best shows I ever worked on was a transfer from Theatre503 that followed this exact pattern. What was it that made me come down to see it? Five stars in The Stage, four stars in The Telegraph and four stars in WhatsOnStage. That's it. Frustrating that, isn't it?! Fear not, casting directors, agents, even artistic directors will all be interested in different elements. For me it's the whole show, for others it's different component parts.

Do invite people to your show. Do be polite. Try not to be offended if they don't come back to you. This is a key part of doing business.

Stage One

Stage One is an organization that supports emerging theatre producers in the UK. They provide a number of schemes including apprenticeships, workshops and bursaries. They are *absolutely* worth talking to, but will only be of limited help once you're into the production process, so talk to them early.

Do apply for their bursary. It's a nice amount of money, and could be used to support you while you produce the show.

If you decide you've got the producing bug (many accidental producers have in the past), then Stage One should be your first port of call for opportunities of apprenticeships, training or commercial investment.

Managing mental health

Producing is hugely engaging and incredibly exciting. It can also be stressful. In particular when it's rushed. I've mentioned a few times that time is your best friend when putting together a show. I cannot emphasize enough how much harder it is when you're rushing. Every single thing in this book becomes tougher when you're tight for time.

A few years ago I signed up to do my biggest show to date. It was my first six-figure budget, and was a big leap that, if successful, would have opened up significant opportunity for me. While the script was established, everything else was starting from scratch. New brand, new cast, new design, everything.

I signed the venue deal on 1 November for a first preview on 11 January. If that doesn't sound insane enough, I was general-managing a show opening that December, and had two other smaller shows opening, one in January and the other in March.

Madness. Every time I read that paragraph, I'm more appalled at my decision-making.

What happened? I was offered an 'opportunity' by a venue that I thought was too good to turn down. I thought that if I didn't take the opportunity there and then, I might never have another one. I was hugely impatient about moving my career forward. And I had a script I loved.

Inevitably, the show was not a success. I remain convinced that had I had a six-month run at it, it could have been. What it did do was turn a busy period (three shows in four months was a *lot* anyway) into a period that it was amazing I even managed to get through.

At the end of it all in April that year I had a breakdown from burnout. It wasn't for another nine months that I was back to being myself and I didn't manage to get on another show for a further eighteen months after that.

I don't want to end this book on a negative note. It was a particularly stupid mistake I made deciding to do that show, at that time, on top of everything else. You're not going to do that. No one else is stupid enough to think they can pull off four shows in four months, including their first West End show. I learned the hard way!

But please try not to rush. Patience is the hardest lesson to learn, and it is one that I'm still working on.

Look after yourself. Make sure you're confident you have the time to deliver the show, and the support around you. Make sure your key team are all pointing in the same direction and are doing the show for the right reasons. And remember it's only theatre, it matters, but not enough to risk your health.

I'm back, and as excited to produce as I've ever been. But only with enough *time* to do a good job.

Summary

If you've gone to all the effort of getting a show on, you owe it to yourself to make sure people know about it, and have been invited to see it.

- Having a show on is the best time to network within the industry – make the most of it.
- Do invite people, don't bug them! Follow up with your best marketing and reviews.

Most importantly:
- Look after yourself.

Final conclusions

Ok. Wow. Breathe.

There's a lot. There really is. This is a not a small undertaking. But all of it is possible. You need to be committed, you need to be organized, you *must* be driven as hell but you *can* do this.

If you take only one thing from this book, take this.

The play's the thing.

Promise me you will embark on this journey only if you love the script. If you love the potential but not the current script, then develop it, but you must sign a venue only when you love it. You can make no bigger mistake than beginning this journey with a script you don't believe in.

There are so many brilliant scripts and so many brilliant writers that you *will* find the perfect one.

My other key takeaways:

- Try to not rush into an opportunity. A year's time may sound a long way away, but you will not regret taking the time. It helps with fundraising, getting the right team and right casting, having a detailed and achievable press, sales and marketing plan, everything. This is easier advice to give than to follow . . .
- Get a great team around you. The choice of director is key. They will be your ally throughout.
- Raise the money before you sign the venue agreement. Or have a financial backup plan.

Finally. Enjoy it.

We make theatre because we love it, there's no other reason. I have found no life experience to match the thrill of the first performance of a show. The reason we do this is for that thrill of telling stories.

Go find the story you want to tell. And start doing it.

Good luck.

Appendix

Case study interview with actor and producer Kevin Shen

Kevin is an American and British actor, writer and producer based in London. His first professional stage role was as the lead in the play *Yellow Face* that he produced at Park Theatre in London, which transferred to the National Theatre the following year. He produced the play with his company Special Relationship Productions, which he founded with fellow actor Lucy Fenton. I advised Kevin and Lucy through the first production and they employed me to general-manage the transfer.

Tim Johanson What was your motivation for wanting to produce?

Kevin Shen There were a lot. For myself as an actor, I didn't go to drama school, so I thought it was a good opportunity to get some work to showcase myself. It was also politically motivated.

I met a director who suggested I help him produce a play. I did so, and thought it was very manageable. At a similar time I passed a major theatre which had a poster of a character who was Asian but seemed to be being played by a white person. I went to the box office and asked if that was the case, and they said, 'yeah, what's wrong with that?' I thought, 'I should produce *Yellow Face*; that is a great play that should be seen, and addresses these issues.'

TJ Had you seen *Yellow Face* at that time?

KS I hadn't. Nor had I read it. But I knew of the writer, David (Henry Hwang), and the premise, and I knew it was well regarded. Then I read it and loved it, and thought there was a great part for me.

So it was both a project for my acting and with political motivations, and having witnessed the producing scene, I worked out it was something I could actually do.

TJ How did you get the rights?

KS Generally in producing, I'd say you try to use all the connections that you have; you reach out and start pulling at everything that you can pull. I went to the same university as David, and had met him at an event a few years before I became an actor, so I looked up his email address on our alumni database and emailed him directly to ask if I could have the rights to his play. And he said sure!

TJ   How was the process with the agent? Was it straightforward
     because David had given the green light? Did you need to have a
     director on board in order to get it signed off?

KS   Well, we came in with this director, with his track record etc. David
     had approval of everything, including cast, which I was nervous
     about because I hadn't mentioned about being in it yet. Then I
     emailed David after, and he was very approachable and supportive;
     he said he trusted the director. Then some issues came up with that
     director, so I emailed asking if we could change directors and find a
     new one, and that was all fine, too.
        I was also worried about venues. I asked him about being at a
     small venue, and he just said 'I love small venues, I think intimate
     venues are great'. We were lucky, he's just down to earth, he doesn't
     have an ego. Despite how narcissistic *Yellow Face* is . . . ! He's
     the chillest writer and super- supportive of up-and-coming Asian-
     Americans. That was extremely helpful – to have a cooperative, easy-
     going, supportive writer, who is well established. It definitely helps
     your future productions, too, when your negotiating stance includes
     'well, David Henry Hwang didn't require that'.

TJ   I would definitely use that. What happened next? Was it a new
     director? Was it the venue?

KS   Lucy and I cold-emailed people, reaching out to anyone. I was
     just starting as an actor, so I didn't have many connections. We were
     just cold-emailing any connection we could find. If there was a name
     that could be dropped, we would drop it, and for the most part,
     artistic directors of theatres were responsive if we said 'Hi, we're new
     producers, we're trying to produce this play, could we have a coffee
     and get some advice?'

TJ   What sort of venues were you after?

KS   Every one. We sat down with Sean Holmes (Artistic Director at the
     Lyric Hammersmith at the time), we sat down with Steve Marmion
     at Soho Theatre; David Lan responded for sure.

TJ   Oh, so you went high.

KS   We just emailed all artistic directors, asking for a coffee. A few
     were connections, but mainly it was cold emails. Also, some people
     don't like to pick up the phone, but I don't mind. So I'd just call
     venues looking for email addresses/contacts. We talked to anyone
     we could in the producing sphere. We were pretty clueless. But
     that cluelessness kind of helped as we didn't know when to censor
     ourselves!
        We were trying to deal with venues for about a year. We got a
     lot of different responses 'nobody knows who DHH is, it's too
     esoteric', or 'no one wants to see a play about Asian-Americans' – we
     got that, too.

TJ   Really?

KS   Yes. Even when I pointed out that his previous play starred
Anthony Hopkins and broke records in the West End.

TJ   So where was Park Theatre at that point?

KS   We didn't go immediately to them, but we knew they were building
the theatre, and we both had a relationship with Jez and Melli,
because Lucy and I met on an acting workshop that Melli ran. We
had quite a good relationship there. So when it was opening, I asked
how I could make this a thing, and she suggested we run a session
at this acting workshop as a reading, so we did that, which went
well. At that point the Park was our only venue we had an open
conversation with.

I then made a PowerPoint presentation for Jez, taking all their
vision and values from their website and showing how *Yellow Face*
fit in. It was timely because the *Orphan of Zhao* controversy was
happening at the RSC right then, *and Miss Saigon* had announced a
revival in the West End. It all felt well-timed, and then Jez had us do
a day-long workshop with him, which I think was basically a day-
long audition for me.

TJ   I remember the presentation and the workshop. So you talked Jez
round and he offered you a slot in the 90?

KS   We had also done readings with other directors. We were trying
to work out if we should find a director to help get the venue. But
nothing landed, and then Jez recommended a couple of directors
that we ended up talking to, and that's how we ended up with Alex
(Simms).

TJ   And how about money?

KS   Well, the numbers just weren't going to make sense as a
commercial venture. It had a break even at 80 per cent capacity, and
we needed to budget at 40 per cent capacity, so it just didn't work. I
suspect now with Park 90 you couldn't have even made it work at 80
per cent, with a properly paid cast of that size. So from then, we were
basically trying to just get donations.

We did a Kickstarter and made £100 or something insignificant.
Then we got a fiscal sponsor in the US, because we were largely
going to my contacts in the US. This provided us with 501c3 status
that you can accept donations to, and they take a fee, so it's like
a crowdfunding source that is tax-deductible. The great thing
about it – as it's a charity – is that you can use employee donation-
matching programmes, so I went to my friends and family and
asked if they could donate money, and their employers would
match it.

TJ   Is that where all the money came from? Plus box office.

KS   Actually just with box office, we would have ended up pretty much
breaking even. We ended up being able to give everyone a bonus at

the end. We also had some associates who had emailed us asking to be involved, but who we had told we couldn't pay as we had no budget for them, but they had wanted to help anyway, and at the end we were able to give them something as well.

TJ In terms of the delivery of the show, was there anything in particular that you were worried about?

KS It was a hard process. It's why I now recommend actor-producers not to self-produce and to find a producer. But I had Lucy. Part of it was the balance between being in it and producing. Initially we were both going to be in it; there was a part for Lucy as well, but a lot of people and venues we approached were not okay with two first-time actor-producers. Lucy graciously stepped back and let me be in it, whilst she was the primary producer, and then we produced another play where we switched roles.

Part of it was that work balance. When we started rehearsals, we were just working to the bone. I would be in rehearsals 10 am to 6 pm and then would be doing producing stuff from 6 pm to 2 am, which doesn't do great things for your performance. At one point the director called Lucy and said she couldn't talk to me anymore, because my performance was suffering and I needed to focus.

We also tried not to have a casting director to begin with, so we were Spotlight-searching, looking up people, watching show reels, the three of us (Alex, Lucy, and me), for hours on end. We realized a casting director was quite important to get a legit response from the agent, and also just to help find the right people. Alex the director was amazing through all of it.

Lucy was doing all the heavy lifting in terms of logistics. We learned marketing costs felt like mostly a waste, apart from PR. Press was a huge thing to get butts on seats. We hired a PR person, who was the Park's person, and she fell ill and had her friend help cover the campaign, who happened to be one of the top theatre PR agents in London, and we got all the broadsheets to come review the show. It was also helpful that we were the first show in the Park's studio space. Getting reviews was important.

Marketing-wise, we did posters in pubs and whatnot, we hired people to distribute flyers, we went ourselves to local restaurants and put posters up. It felt like anything you had to pay for did not seem to have a great return on investment.

TJ Was there stuff you didn't have to pay for that you felt worked?

KS We used social media and did that all ourselves. I targeted everybody who'd seen Chimerica and tweeted about it, responding with something like 'here's another show you might enjoy about race'.

There was also a promotion going on in Chinatown, by a group called the British Chinese Project. I talked to one of the women who was there, and she introduced me to the guy who was running the project. He ended up doing our Chinese PR and made all the connections with the Chinese language media.

We gave him a 'Chinese' press night, which was in addition to our usual press night, where we had all the Chinese press come in, plus all the people from his organization. We didn't pay him a fee, but gave him in-kind support through promotion and the back page of our programme. It all came from pulling someone over on the street to talk to!

TJ   What was the hardest bit of it?

KS   It was generally very hard – balancing being in it with all the producing. I didn't quite realize how demanding it would be as an actor. But also there's just a lot of stuff that has to get done. Especially when it's just the two of you, or when it was just Lucy, by herself. We were doing as much in-house as we could, to save money, so all the image design, all the programmes, we didn't hire very many people at all. It was all so time-consuming. And we didn't know a lot, so we were learning on the fly as well.

TJ   Did you hire a production manager?

KS   No. It was Lucy. She's a hero.

TJ   No wonder she was so tired. It was Lily Arnold who designed it, right? What did she think about not having a production manager?! It's the number one thing I tell people to find.

KS   She had . . . Lucy. Who was managing the money. We couldn't afford another person to help.

It's just got to be something you're super-passionate about, because you are selling it to every person you talk to. And it helps to have a great script. With David Yip, who was in the cast, I had talked to him previously, and then I took him to lunch and told him about the play. We had to adjust rehearsals to accommodate him; I think he started a couple of days late. Gemma (Chan) just loved the play as well.

TJ   Getting her was a real coup, wasn't it? Because she was breaking out.

KS   Yeah it was very helpful.

Our sound designer was Isobel Waller-Bridge, our designer was Lily Arnold, lighting was by Josh Carr. They were at that point mostly doing fringe theatre I believe. I think it was everyone's first show at the National, and now they're all much more successful than I am!

Finding good talent, getting a good script and believing in it as a project are key. If you don't, then no one will. You're just putting so much time into it, and you're not getting paid for it, or not much. You've got to love it.

TJ Thinking about my shows, it took me to about my ninth project before I was the most passionate person doing it. It took me almost ten years to work out that the producer has to be more passionate than everyone else. The producer is there at the beginning and there at the end.

KS Right, and their whole job is to sell it. If you don't love it, it's not going to happen. If you can talk about it out your ears, and I still can about *Yellow Face*, it was just so easy to pitch to anyone I talk to.

TJ What would be your advice to you back then?

KS My advice now is hire a general manager. Hire someone to do the work, who knows how to do the work. But it's hard when you don't have that in your budget. The person who's going to do the most for free is you.

TJ Ok, so would you go back and not do it?

KS No, no, definitely not, no.

TJ So your advice isn't don't do it?

KS It's get someone to help you do it!

TJ Did it achieve what you wanted?

KS Absolutely. It achieved what we wanted from a political perspective, from a career perspective, from an artistic perspective. It achieved more than we wanted. We did not think we'd transfer to the National with it. That was beyond anyone's expectations. We personally called the whole cast to tell them we were transferring. It was one of the most fun days ever.

TJ Would you repeat it?

KS I think if the situations were right . . . but I'd do it where we could hire someone. We did it for Lucy's play, where we hired a GM to come work for us.

TJ What about from you as an actor then, rather than as a producer? In terms of you and your career? If an actor came to you and said, 'I'm struggling to get shifting', would you say to them, 'Have you thought about finding a script for yourself?'

KS Good question. I guess it depends on the actor. I know other actors who've done it and done really well for themselves. It's a great showcase, if it's a good play, but it is a lot of work.

There are tons of actors who are super-scrappy and ambitious who can do it, especially when you're in your twenties. You have that invincibility. Now that I'm a bit older I'm a bit more jaded and cynical! Back when I was doing *Yellow Face*, no problem. I like to reference this Orson Welles story, where he was asked something like 'Citizen Kane is so revolutionary, how were you able to do it, how did you know you could use all these revolutionary film techniques?'

and he basically responded, 'It was my first film, I didn't know what I couldn't do.'

Just go for it. Actors are doing it all the time, making short films or whatever. If you have the ambition and the drive and the energy, then yes, go for it.

INDEX